D0070223

DANGEROUS PURSUITS

ALSO BY WALTER ADAMS AND JAMES BROCK

The Bigness Complex

OTHER BOOKS BY WALTER ADAMS

The Structure of American Industry

Monopoly in America: The Government as Promoter

Trucking Mergers, Concentration and Small Business

From Mainstreet to the Left Bank

Is the World Our Campus?

A Guide to Study Abroad

The Brain Drain

The Test

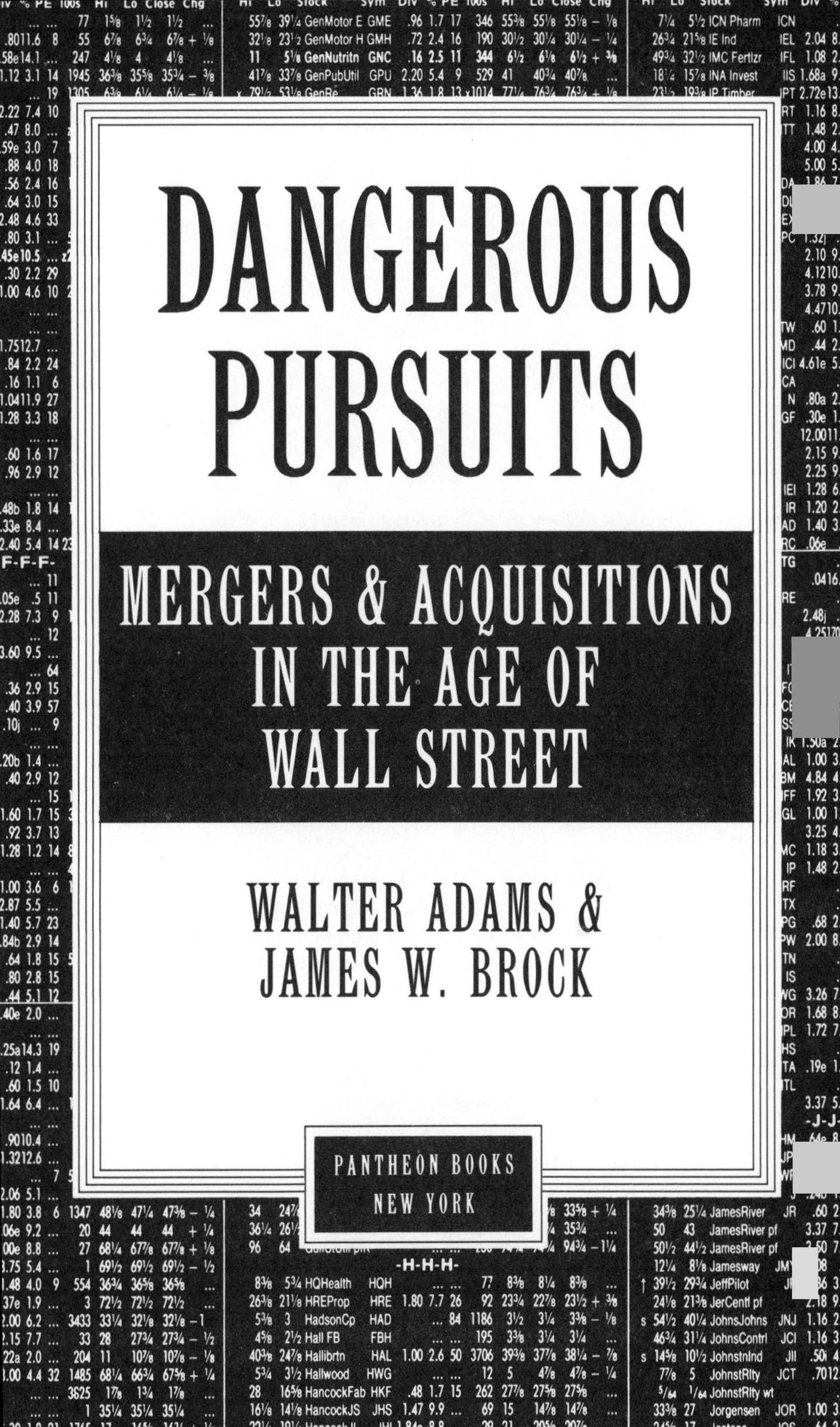

DANGEROUS PURSUITS

MERGERS & ACQUISITIONS IN THE AGE OF WALL STREET

WALTER ADAMS &
JAMES W. BROCK

PANTHEON BOOKS
NEW YORK

 Published in the United States by Pantheon Books, a division of Random House, Inc., New York, and simultaneously in Canada by Random House of Canada Limited, Toronto.

Grateful acknowledgment is made to Dow Jones & Company, Inc., for permission to adapt a chart from Street Scene by Stewart, Burrough, & Swartz from *The Wall Street Journal*, February 3, 1988.

LIBRARY OF CONGRESS CATALOGING-IN-PUBLICATION DATA

Adams, Walter, 1922 Aug. 27-

Dangerous pursuits : mergers and acquisitions in the age of Wall Street / Walter Adams and James W. Brock. — 1st ed.

p. cm.

Bibliography: p.

Includes Index.

ISBN 0-394-57967-4

1. Consolidation and merger of corporations—United States.

I. Brock, James W. II. Title.

HD2785.A686 1989

338.8'3'0973—dc20 89-42653

Designed by Beth Tondreau Design

Manufactured in the United States of America

First Edition

CONTENTS

IV. THE ALTERNATIVES

V. A REAPPRAISAL

TO ENTREPRENEURS
AND INNOVATORS
WHO PLAY
THE RIGHT GAME

PREFACE

To Americans, a casino is a gambling emporium—a Las Vegas or Atlantic City establishment for crapshooters, roulette players, and baccarat addicts.

To Italians, a casino is a house of ill repute—an establishment where specialists practice the world's oldest profession.

Today, the contest for corporate control in America features elements of both—greed and lust.

The arena is Wall Street, where America's business elite is playing this game with ferocious intensity and monomaniacal obsession.

The game takes several forms: mergers, acquisitions, takeovers, and buyouts.

The participating players are diverse and numerous: There are the establishmentarians—members of the Business Roundtable, leaders of the very largest American corporations—who want to protect their fiefdoms from usurpers and *arrivistes*. There are the counter-establishmentarians—the "raiders," the "gunslingers"—who want to oust somnolent rulers from the pinnacles of industrial power. There are the leveraged buyout specialists who want to save the corporations they manage by dismembering them. There are the dealbrokers, Wall Street's investment bankers, who arrange corporate marriages as well as divorces. There is the supporting cast of mercenaries—lawyers, accountants, economists, consultants, arbitrageurs, and mavens—who help to keep the game going. Finally, there is the inchoate chorus of stockholders and stakeholders, bondholders and creditors, who are part players and part spectators in a fast-moving, multicornered contest.

It is not a traditional game. Its essence is the trading of corporate ownership titles rather than investment in new plant and equipment, or in research and development, or in net capital formation. It most resembles the game of musical chairs. Avis, for example, has had ten different owners in three decades. Founded in 1946 by Warren Avis, it was sold to a Hertz licensee in 1954, to a group of Boston investors in 1956, to the investment bankers Lazard Freres in 1962, and to ITT in 1965. Spun off to ITT stockholders in 1973, it was acquired by Norton Simon in 1977, by Esmark (which acquired Norton Simon) in 1983, by Beatrice (which acquired Esmark) in 1984, by Kohlberg Kravis Roberts (which bought out Beatrice) in 1985, by Wesray Capital Corp. (William Simon's investment firm) in 1986, and finally by Avis employees (in an ESOP buyout) in 1987. A profitable game, perhaps, for the players, but hardly an adventure in creative capitalism.

The game has another side—popular fascination. Headlines chronicle its progress, reporting deal-by-deal details and day-to-day rumors: "Year of the Mega Deals Is Upon Us"; "The Billion-Dollar Buyout"; "Corporate America Snuggles Up to the Buyout Wolves"; "A Game of Greed."

There are the predictable questions about winners and losers: "The Feeding Frenzy Has Its Price"; "Pillsbury's President Will Make Tidy Profit on Takeover, Even As Earnings Sag"; "Sir James Goldsmith Collects $90 Million in Greenmail"; "Investment Bankers Should Get at Least $386.3 Million in RJR Nabisco Buyout."

There are lurid accounts about cheaters to titillate prurient interests: "Boesky Goes to Jail"; "Levine Cooperates with Investigators"; "U.S. Indicts Singer's Bilzerian in Raids on 3 Firms"; "Superstar Lawyer Sentenced for Insider Trading"; "Drexel Burnham Lambert Pleads Guilty; Agrees to Pay Out a Record $650 Million."

Then, of course, there is concern about the consequences of the game: "Why the RJR Circus Is So Dangerous"; "Takeover Trend

Helps Push Corporate Debt and Defaults Upward"; "For Business, the Thrills and Chills of Living with Debt"; "Impact on R&D Is Newest Worry About LBO's"; "Slow Rise in Outlays for Research Imperils U.S. Competitive Edge"; "Philip Morris Merger with Kraft May Limit Product Innovation"; "America in Decline"; "Is Big Business Its Own Worst Enemy?"

Beyond these concerns there is a more basic unease that the game is being played under ominous clouds on the financial horizon: a national debt of $2.3 trillion, with interest payments accounting for 14 percent of government expenditures. A corporate debt at $1.8 trillion and rising steadily. An annual budget deficit around $150 billion which neither Congress, nor the White House, nor the two working together seems able to bring under control. A trade deficit narrowing ever so slowly despite a decimated dollar. A credit-card prosperity, at least for the vast majority of Americans, financed largely with the savings of foreigners. And America—not some Third World or East Bloc country—the largest debtor nation in the world.[1]

Buried in these dismal statistics is a record of inadequate capital formation and sluggish productivity growth. President Reagan diagnosed this structural problem early in his first administration: "Today this once great industrial giant of ours has the lowest gain in productivity of virtually all the industrial countries with whom we need to compete in the world market." He called for massive investment in new plants and equipment in order to modernize production facilities and enhance the average worker's output. With productivity on the rise again, the president said, our standard of living would once again begin to climb.

Alas, the response to this challenge was spectacularly unimpressive. While net business capital formation averaged 3 percent of total income in the 1950s, 3.5 percent during the 1960s, and 3.3 percent during the 1970s, it has averaged just 2.3 percent so far during the 1980s. "In no single year since 1981," says economist Benjamin Friedman, "have we achieved over 3 percent."[2] The difference may seem small, but its compounded effect is substantial. As Princeton economist Alan S. Blinder points out, "At 2 percent annual growth, real wages double every thirty-five years; in a century, the standard of living increases more than sevenfold. But at 1 percent productivity growth, it takes seventy years for real wages to double, and the standard of living less than triples in a century. Clearly, restoring U.S. productivity growth to its historic 2 percent norm would be a monumental achievement."[3]

The problem can be ignored only at our peril. As the MIT Commission on Industrial Productivity noted in its comprehensive report, "other indicators of industrial performance that are less easily quantified than productivity but no less important tell a disquieting story. In such areas as product quality, service to customers, and speed of product development, American companies are no longer perceived as world leaders, even by American consumers. There is also evidence that technological innovations are being incorporated more quickly abroad, and [that] the pace of invention and discovery in the United States may be slowing."[4]

Nevertheless, the merger game has enthusiastic advocates and afficionados. "Merger activity in general," said William F. Baxter, President Reagan's first chief of the Justice Department's Antitrust Division, "is a very important feature of our capital markets by which assets are continuously moved into the hands of managers who can employ them efficiently." Interfering with mergers "would be an error of substantial magnitude." "Bigness doesn't necessarily mean badness," said Attorney General William French Smith. A more liberal attitude to mergers would "make the United States more competitive," said his successor Edwin Meese III. "The world economy has changed," averred Commerce Secretary Malcolm Baldrige. "Trade patterns have changed, but the antitrust laws have not. It is not that some parts of those laws are irrelevant today; it is the fact that they place additional and unnecessary burdens on the ability of U.S. firms to compete." In short, merger-induced restructuring is absolutely imperative if American industry is to achieve production efficiency, technological innovation, and competitiveness in world markets.

In this book we shall explore the current addiction to mergeritis. We shall examine the dynamics of the game, the reasons for playing it, the role of the players, and its consequences. Most important, we shall inquire whether it makes any sense and what, if anything, we ought to do about it. Do mergers indeed promote efficiency, technical progress, and international competitiveness, or are they an exercise in sterile financial razzle-dazzle? Is it sensible to embark on a frenzied acquisition binge today only to divest the acquired assets one year, five years, or ten years later? Are the marriage brokers who arrange corporate unions, and then preside over the subsequent divorces (for generous fees at both ends), performing an economically productive service? Is it rational for American business to spend more on mergers and acquisitions than on research and development and new plant and equipment combined?

In short, are we (and the Europeans who seem to be following our example) playing the right game? Or, are we trying to excel at a game that we should not be playing at all? (As Peter Drucker reminds us, it's one thing to be efficient—"doing things right." It's quite another to be effective—"doing the right things.")

In a free enterprise economy, a recurrent restructuring of corporations is both normal and healthy. However, as ITT chairman Rand Araskog points out, the current merger mania "has more to do with the self-fulfilling prophecies of some egomaniacal financiers and overwhelming ambition of some investment houses than with business efficiencies. Too many deals are being done because of the ability to do them—not because they have sound economic logic or business validity." It's a game that has gotten out of control.

"Our nation is rushing blindly to the precipice," says Martin Lipton, the Park Avenue lawyer and veteran of the merger game, who reportedly received the largest fee in history in connection with a corporate consolidation. "As with tulip bulbs, South Sea bubbles, pyramid investment trusts, Florida land, REITs, LDC loans, Texas banks and all other financial market frenzies of the past, the denouement will be a crash."[5]

If or when this happens, will merger-bloated companies "that took on massive debt be allowed to fail, even if that would threaten to worsen the business contraction?" asks Henry Kaufman, the highly respected and influential Wall Streeter. "Or will there be a clamor for a safety net, a lender of last resort in the form of a government bailout," thus putting "the government into the business of business"—to the detriment of "the health of the free enterprise system"?[6]

This view may be unduly pessimistic, especially in the midst of general prosperity when Americans "feel good" about themselves and their country. We have enjoyed eight successive years of near full employment without double-digit interest rates and without double-digit inflation. In spite of a crushing debt burden, the sky hasn't fallen and the nation prospers. And, says a *New York Times* editorial, "Politicians, financiers and academics now dare to think the unthinkable: Could it be that deficits don't matter after all?"[7]

When an airplane functions, with apparent efficiency and only minor mishaps, one seldom inquires into its structural properties or the principles of aerodynamics. Yet, it is precisely when everything seems to be going well that analytical inquiry may be both necessary and rewarding. The citizens of ancient Rome, Edward Gibbon reminds us, were once blinded by a general aura of "public felicity" and therefore unaware of "a slow and secret poison" seeping into "vitals of the empire." The decline and eventual fall of the empire, he writes, was "the natural and inevitable effect of immoderate success. Prosperity ripened the principle of decay; the causes of destruction multiplied with the extent of conquest; and as soon as time or accident had removed the artificial supports, the stupendous fabric yielded to the pressure of its own weight. The story of its ruin is simple and obvious; and instead of inquiring *why* the Roman empire was destroyed, we should rather be surprised that it had subsisted so long."[8]

June 1989
Le Val Majour, Fontvieille

WALTER ADAMS
JAMES W. BROCK

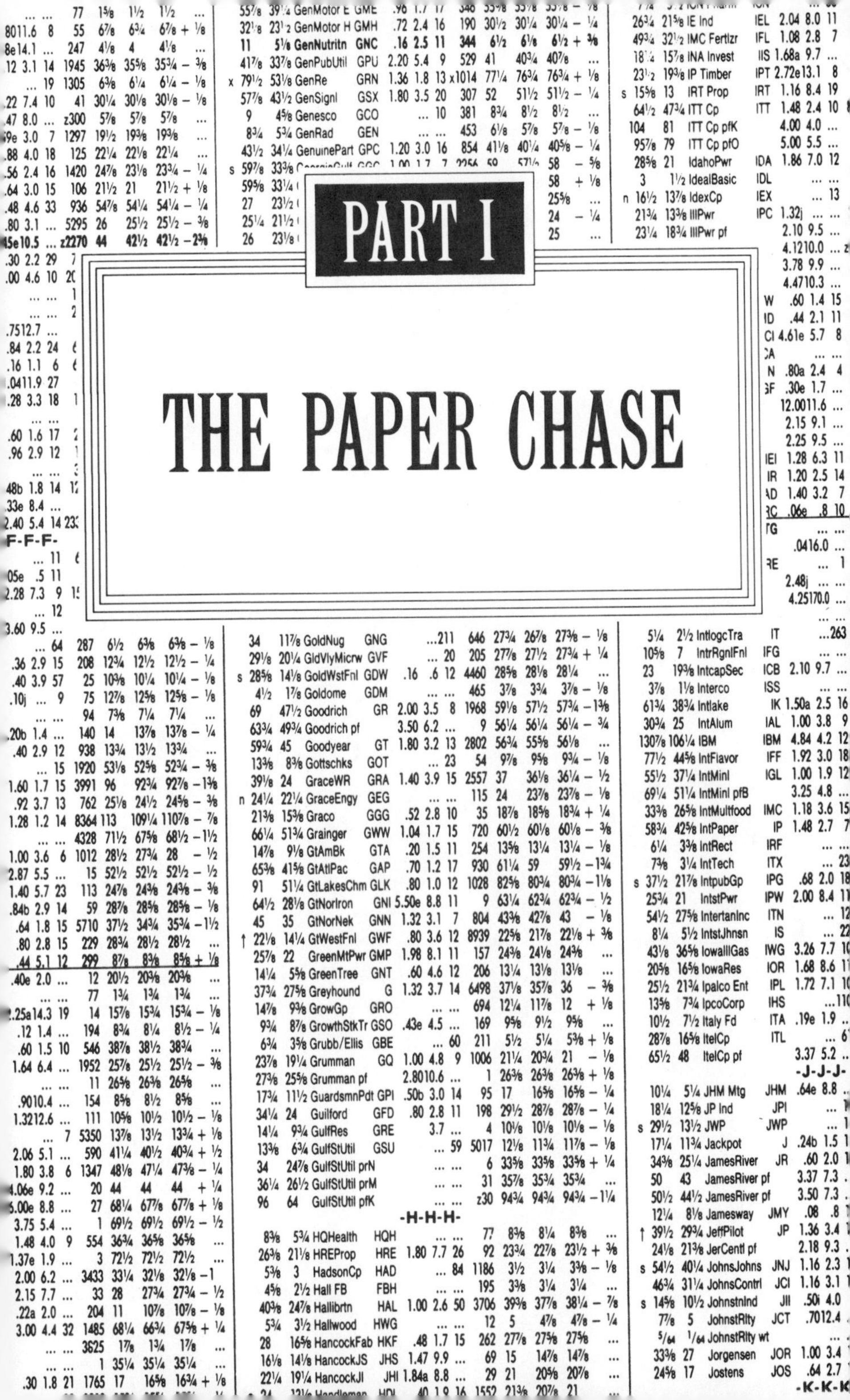

PART I

THE PAPER CHASE

1 THE GAME

In battle or business, whatever the game,
In law or in love, it is ever the same;
In the struggle for power, or the scramble for pelf,
Let this be your motto—
Rely on yourself!
—John Godfrey Saxe,
"The Games of Life"

These days, the incantation is "money, money, money," says *Fortune*. "Bewitched by an epidemic of money enchantment, Americans in the eighties wriggle in a St. Vitus dance of materialism unseen since the Gilded Age or the Roaring Twenties. Under the blazing sun of money, all other values shine palely. And the M&A decade acclaims but one breed of hero: He's the honcho with the condo and the limo and the Miro and lots of dough."[1] In the Roaring Eighties, the merger game—deal-making of all sorts—is the hottest game in town.

Games, psychotherapists tell us, are a response to "stimulus-hunger" in infants and "sensory deprivation" in adults. They satisfy a pervasive "structure-hunger"—the need to avoid boredom. A form of social intercourse, games help to dispel apathy and anomie, especially in large-scale settings. Unless they are destructive in nature, games contribute to an individual's mental health and social adjustment.

Games come in all varieties. There are children's games (ring-around-the-rosie) and adult games (masquerades). There are card games (pinochle), parlor games (charades), party games (hopscotch), and athletic games (football). There are fun games (pin-the-tail-on-the-donkey), serious games (chess), and deadly games (war). There are games of chance, games of wit, and games of skill.

Games involve a stereotyped series of moves or gimmicks, following prescribed procedures and rituals, and aimed to achieve a specified outcome (payoff). They entail detailed practical planning, and success depends on virtuosity in executing the prescribed maneuvers. In essence, games are a theatrical surrogate for reality, a sublimation of combat in lifelike (yet fictional) settings.

A prototypical game is the athletic event. It is a colorful spectacle, a folkloric pageant, a Roman circus. Played with grim determination, it may or may not be "fun" for the players. But it generates tension and suspense, thrills and chills, exhilaration and excitement. It satisfies the appetite of the roaring crowd.

The rules are strictly prescribed: the dimensions of the playing field, the size of the teams, the way to score, the duration of the contest.

There are various offensive maneuvers: line plunges, forward passes, reverses, statue-of-liberty plays, draw plays, fake punts.

There is a panoply of defensive maneuvers: the man-to-man defense, the zone defense, the nickel defense, double coverage, the blitz.

There are sanctions against violations of the rules (offside, clipping, spearing, interference, unnecessary roughness), as well as multiple arbiters to enforce the rules and impose penalties (referees, umpires, line judges, back judges, timekeepers).

There is a clear objective. In the immortal words of Vince Lombardi: "Winning is not the most important thing. It is the only thing."

The formal ritual on the field is matched by an equally formal ritual on the sidelines. There are teams of cheerleaders to exhort the faithful; the mass shouting of organized slogans; the blare of band music; obscenities (and, at times, more formidable objects) hurled at the referees—all in an atmosphere of frenzied hoopla and orchestrated mass hysteria.

Off the field, there is an impressive cast of supporting players. A platoon of coaches (offensive and defensive coordinators, backfield and line coaches, physical conditioning coaches, and scouts) develop strategy and come up with a suitable game plan.

There are organized leagues, and high commissioners (veritable czars) to impose structure on the game. They prescribe season schedules, the rules for playoffs, tournaments, and bowl games, as well as regulations for player eligibility and conduct. They also mediate disputes among team owners, and between team owners and the players' associations.

There are sportswriters, broadcasters, public relations operatives, oddsmakers, rumormongers, gurus, gamblers, and mavens to analyze an upcoming contest and to generate din, hype, and excitement.

There is a cash nexus: the television networks and the commercial sponsors who help defray the costs of the game (over and above the proceeds from "live" admissions); the cities that are conned into building palatial stadiums to attract "home" teams and engage in constant competition to retain them; the owners of a franchise who are sportsmen with a keen appreciation of the profit-maximization calculus; the players' agents who market "human capital" to the highest bidders.

Beyond these realities, however, is the mythology surrounding the game—the symbols which make it a popular attraction. For social approbation, it is indispensable to establish that the game in question is quintessentially American and that it is a primordial expression of American values and American culture. In baseball, the Atlanta Braves call themselves "America's Team"; in football, this sobriquet is claimed by the Dallas Cowboys. (Dallas now is *really*

America's team; the FDIC has wound up owning 12 percent of the Cowboys—the result of a Texas bank bailout.)

Most games, as Yogi Berra would say, are over when they are over. In the larger scheme of things, their outcome is inconsequential. The battle may have been arduous, the contest impassioned, but when the final whistle blows, players and spectators alike know that it was only a game. Reality returns, dispelling myth and make-believe.

Deal-making is a different sort of game. Its consequences are anything but trivial, and its ramifications extend beyond the particular deal. The ripple effects have an impact not only on the participants involved, but on entire industries and the national economy—their efficiency, their technological progressiveness, their international competitiveness, and the standard of living. Deal-making is more than just a run-of-the-mill game.

What makes deal-making fascinating, and frightening, are the stupendous, multibillion-dollar sums wagered, the jobs and economic livelihoods at stake, and the shifting, twisting mix of otherwise familiar sports it presents, with players, tactics, and teams careening from deal to deal, and from one field of play to another. As Alice remarked about the croquet game, "I don't think they play at all fairly—and they don't seem to have any rules in particular; at least if there are any, nobody attends to them."

The game board is corporate America—manufacturing, commerce, finance, transportation, and utilities. Coast to coast, North to South, wheat belt to rust belt, and mountain states to Manhattan, the field is coterminous with the country at large. Recently, it has come to include the entire industrialized free world.

The players come in all shapes and sizes. Some play the game in a multiplicity of roles, sometimes simultaneously, sometimes in a succession of deals. Outside raiders—T. Boone Pickens, Saul Steinberg, Ronald Perelman, and Carl Icahn—mount attacks to take over target firms, to control them, and then to keep them or to split them up and sell them off in pieces packaged to appeal to yet other buyers.

Corporate managements play the game in a number of ways, sometimes voluntarily, sometimes under duress. Some managements struggle grimly to defeat raids by hostile outsiders. Other managements are inside raiders: They borrow huge sums; they acquire equity control of the firms they manage; then they take their firms "private" through leveraged buyouts. Some managements play the game by acquiring other firms in friendly deals, or by serving as "white knights" to rescue them from the clutches of a hostile raider, or by launching hostile raids of their own. Some managements even combine these roles by acquiring investment banks, and by consolidating their own industrial operations with those of investment banks that finance the corporate deals of others (such as General Electric's acquisition of the investment bank Kidder Peabody in 1986).

Investment banks and lenders stake the players. They provide the financial fuel. They raise the billions required to finance mergers, raids, and leveraged buyouts. They support the players from the sidelines by coaching them, and by marketing their stocks and bonds—services for which they are handsomely paid. Increasingly, these financial intermediaries have become major players in their own right, contriving and then peddling corporate deals that they hope will continue to capture revenues and fees for them. In fact, they play a game within the game—vying against one another to handle deals, to substitute their own deals for those underwritten by their rivals, and to protect (and extend) their turf. Ironically, employee pension funds—run for workers of states and corporations who, in turn, decry job and income losses from corporate deal-mania—also have become important financial players, providing billions to fund the operations of leveraged-buyout firms like Kohlberg Kravis Roberts.

Stock traders and shareholders play too. Traders thrive on the chaos and price gyrations generated by deal-mania in the stock exchanges and bond markets. Arbitrageurs relentlessly search out potential takeover candidates because, if these firms are "put into play" as takeover targets, their stocks will skyrocket in value. Acquiring large blocks of stock with lightning speed, "arbs" like Ivan Boesky can affect the outcomes of deals decisively, depending on which of the combatants they choose to sell out to. Investment banks play dual roles—running stock trading and stock arbitrage operations on the one side, and handling (and facilitating) merger-mania on the other. Other traders, angling for a small piece of these potential jackpots, intently follow the arbs—another game within a game.

Tactics and strategies twist and turn in dialectical fashion. Plays are devised and executed in corporate boardrooms, at the headquarters of banks and law firms, at combat field sites and in swank hotels, in the stock exchanges and bond markets, through public relations releases and newspaper reports, as well as in the courts and in Congress. At times, the play is straightforward and friendly. More often, the game is closer to warfare—a no-holds-barred combination of boxing, basketball, and checkers, replete with feigned moves and countermoves; full court presses and fast breaks; bluster, bravado, and hand-to-hand combat—but with no fixed rules, no fixed number of players to a team, and no boundaries to the playing field. Field managers of one side in a deal may turn up on the other side in the next deal. Teams and sides change. The field of play leaps from stock markets, to banks, to arbs, to the courts, and back again. The players grow in number at one point, and dwindle at another. At times, one cannot tell the players, even with a scorecard.

Raiders—and their financial and legal advisers—develop two-tiered tender offers designed to defeat management. They stampede stockholders into selling out quickly by offering more for shares sold early than for those sold later in the deal. Managements—and their legal and financial advisers—retaliate by executing "scorched earth," "poison pill," and "shark repellent" strategies designed to deter raids. They lay "minefields" and "booby traps" to cripple the target firm in the event of a successful takeover. They incur huge debts to pay special dividends; they revise corporate bylaws to enable stockholders to acquire shares in the merged firm at ruinously low prices; they unleash blizzards of new shares to prevent raiders from raising their percentage control of the firm's equity; and they nullify voting rights for stocks acquired by raiders.

Managements also implement "lockup options" to defeat raids by contracting in advance to sell especially valuable corporate operations to third parties in the event of an outside takeover. Raiders, in turn, file suits challenging the legality of these management stratagems, and the game jumps into the courts and into the laps of befuddled jurists. Managements counterattack by taking their case to Congress, and by lobbying states to enact antitakeover laws. The raiders challenge the constitutionality of state antitakeover laws. Meanwhile, target firms transform themselves from victims into aggressors with "Pac-Man" strategies—they launch counteroffers to take over those who initiated the raid!

The pieces moved and countermoved across the game board are companies, factories, operating divisions, jobs, stocks, and bonds. The broad boundaries for these maneuvers are set by three types of game rules. *Security laws* are designed to guard against fraud in the financial marketplace. They apply to corporate deals by specifying the kinds of information that must be publicly disclosed, who must disclose it, when it must be disclosed, who may trade on it, and who may not. *Tax laws* affect the game by specifying the sorts of business expenses that can be deducted from corporate income and therefore are exempt from taxation. For example, interest expenses to service debt can be deducted, whereas dividend payments to stockholders are effectively taxed twice—first as income received by the firm, and then as income received by the stockholder. Tax laws also allow losses from prior years to be carried forward (and future earnings to be carried back) on the company's profit-and-loss statement, and thus can be used to shelter corporate income and protect it from taxation. (For example, when a highly profitable firm purchases another firm with equally sizable losses, the buyer may be able to reduce its tax liability to zero.) *Antitrust laws*, when government chooses to enforce them, prohibit mergers and acquisitions whose effect may be to "substantially lessen competition" or "tend to create a monopoly in any line of commerce in any section of the country." All these rules of the game can be maneuvered and manipulated, in thrust and parry, lawsuit and countersuit, to alter the outcome of the game.

What is the ultimate end of the game? Money. More money. And still more. The transcendent object is not to win this takeover or that merger; it is to make money on the outcome. "Winning" control of this corporation or "losing" control of it to someone else is, in the larger scheme of things, essentially irrelevant. In the final analysis it is the monetary tally that counts. A raider can win by losing if he buys stock in the target firm early and at a low price, and sells out later at a vastly higher price. He can get "greenmail" just for agreeing to desist from further attacks on a target company. A corporate acquirer can be "defeated" by a white knight, and fail to gain control of a targeted victim, but win by making millions on the sale of the target's stock it has acquired. Management can lose control if an outside raid succeeds, but win from golden parachutes that trigger multimillion-dollar severance bonuses, lifetime salaries, and even home mortgage buybacks. Leveraged-buyout operators extol the virtues of taking companies private and putting ownership of firms in the hands of those who manage them, then later reissue stock in order to take the firms public again (sometimes only months after the initial buyout).

The point of the game is profit. But as befits so bizarre a game, it is a peculiar kind of profit: *profit without production*. The game is played not to enhance manufacturing efficiency and productivity, not for research, development, and technological innovation, not to expand jobs for workers and raise the national standard of living, but in order to make profit for the players. Profit from intrigue. Profit from cunning and financial chicanery. Profit from threat, bluff, and counterattack. Profit from shuffling paper ownership shares. But above all else, profit without the burden of producing durable, tangible, real economic wealth.

2

THE SCOREBOARD

Poor, dear God. Playing Idiot's Delight. The game that never means anything, and never ends.

—Robert Emmet Sherwood,
Idiot's Delight

The 1980s is a decade of corporate deals—record-breaking, multibillion-dollar deals to fuse corporations or to break them apart in friendly deals and raider deals. There are buyout deals to take companies private, and "reverse" buyouts to take them public again. Some deals feature luminaries in corporate America, others are deals between unknowns. There are takeover deals by domestic firms; raids by foreigners; horizontal, vertical, and conglomerate deals. It is a paper chase of debt, equity, tender offers, and leverage.

Statistics tell the story. The merger and acquisitions game exploded from 1,565 deals in 1980, having a combined value of $33 billion, to 4,323 deals valued at $204.4 billion in 1986 (Table 1). This represents a threefold increase in the number of mergers and acquisitions, and a spectacular 500 percent increase in the dollar amounts involved. Individual deals valued at $1 billion or more skyrocketed from 3 in 1980 to 34 in 1986. In all, some 26,000 M&A transactions were consummated in the 1980–1988 period, totaling

TABLE 1

CORPORATE MERGERS AND ACQUISITIONS
1980–1988

Year	Number of Mergers and Acquisitions	Value ($ billions)	Number Valued in Excess of $1 billion
1980	1,565	$ 33.0	3
1981	2,326	67.3	8
1982	2,296	60.4	9
1983	2,387	52.8	7
1984	3,158	126.0	19
1985	3,428	145.4	26
1986	4,323	204.4	34
1987	3,701	167.5	30
1988	3,487	226.6	42
TOTAL	26,671	$1,083.4	178

Sources: *Mergers & Acquisitions,* May–June 1989; Walter Adams and James W. Brock, "Reaganomics and the Transmogrification of Merger Policy," *Antitrust Bulletin,* Summer 1988, Table 1, p. 310; U.S. Congress, House, Subcommittee on Labor Management Relations, *Report: Pensions and Leveraged Buyouts,* February 7, 1989.

more than a *trillion* dollars in value—a deal-mania unmatched in American economic history (Chart 1). The biggest, best-known corporations in the country are embroiled in the rambunctious, twisting, turning game (Table 2).

In 1982, for example, the American steel industry was mired in its worst slump since the Great Depression. It was suffering record plant closings and the highest rate of unemployment since records began to be kept in 1933. Having failed to invest in state-of-the-art production technology in the post-World War II period, American steel had steadily fallen behind the rest of the world. By 1982, its losses were running in excess of $3.5 billion annually. The United States Steel Corporation's losses alone were $852 million, with the firm losing $92 on every ton of steel it sold. In terms of capital

CHART 1

NUMBER OF MERGERS 1895–1987

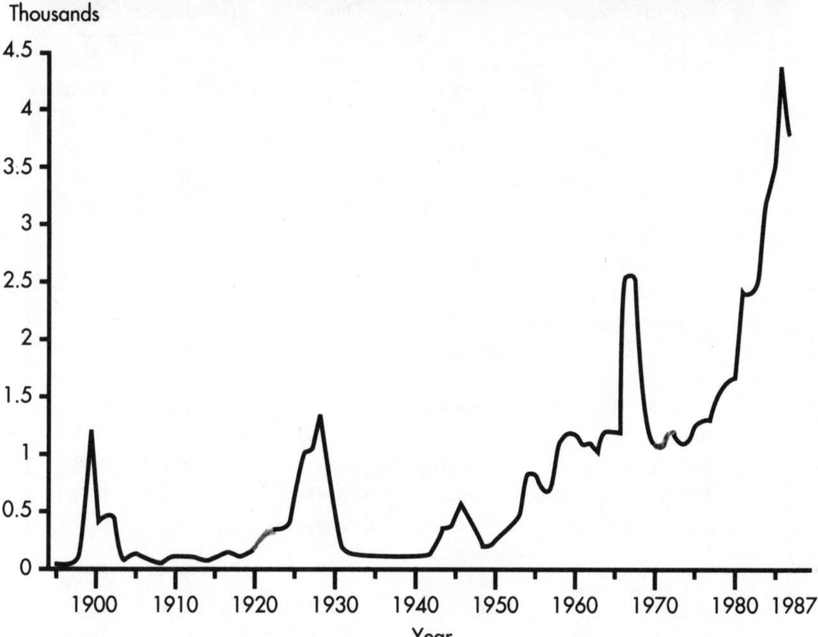

Source: Barrie A. Wigmore, "Speculation and the Crash of 1987." Paper delivered at the annual meeting of the American Economic Association, New York City, December 28, 1988.

TABLE 2

TWENTY LARGEST CORPORATE DEALS IN U.S. HISTORY

Rank and Firms	Type of Deal	Value ($ billions)	Year
1. RJR-Nabisco	Leveraged buyout	$25.0	1989
2. Philip Morris-Kraft	Merger	13.4	1988
3. Chevron-Gulf	Merger	13.3	1984
4. Texaco-Getty	Merger	10.1	1984
5. Du Pont-Conoco	Merger	8.0	1981
6. British Petroleum-Standard Oil	Acquired half-interest not already owned	8.0	1987
7. Campeau-Federated Department Stores	Merger	7.4	1988
8. U.S. Steel-Marathon Oil	Merger	6.6	1982
9. General Electric-RCA	Merger	6.4	1986
10. Beatrice Foods	Leveraged buyout	6.2	1986
11. Royal Dutch Shell-Shell Oil	Acquired one-third interest not already owned	5.7	1985
12. Mobil Oil-Superior	Merger	5.7	1984
13. Philip Morris-General Foods	Merger	5.6	1985
14. Grand Metropolitan-Pillsbury	Merger	5.5	1988
15. Sante Fe-Southern Pacific	Merger	5.1	1983
16. Kodak-Sterling Drug	Merger	5.1	1988
17. Allied-Signal Companies	Merger	4.9	1985
18. R.J. Reynolds-Nabisco	Merger	4.9	1985
19. Burroughs-Sperry	Merger	4.8	1986
20. General Motors-Hughes Aircraft	Merger	4.7	1985

Source: Various business publications, various years.

outlays, Japanese firms were outspending American firms at a rate of 2 to 1.

For a decade and a half, Big Steel had pleaded, cajoled, and lobbied Washington for government protection from more efficient, more innovative foreign producers. U.S. Steel led the political assaults not only in demanding government restraints on steel imports, but in pleading for delays in environmental regulations, as well as in demanding special tax breaks. The avowed reason was that Big Steel desperately needed "breathing space" and funds in order to modernize antiquated plants and facilities and to reindustrialize itself for global competitiveness. In fact, United States Steel Corporation seriously considered buying slab steel from abroad because, it claimed, it lacked the funds to update its domestic plants.

But in the midst of all of this, what did the company proceed to do? It miraculously found $6 billion to acquire Marathon Oil, in a consolidation between the nation's 19th and 39th largest industrial concerns. Two years later, in 1984, U.S. Steel spent another $505 million to acquire Canada's Husky Oil Ltd. And in 1986, U.S. Steel found yet another $3.6 billion to acquire the Texas Oil & Gas Corporation, bringing its combined expenditures for oil and gas mergers to more than $10 billion. It literally transformed itself into an oil company while its frustrated workers complained: "We can't even get money for steel-plant repairs."

Also in 1982, the nation was treated to the spectacle of the four-way feeding frenzy between Bendix, Martin Marietta, United Technologies, and Allied Corporation—the nation's 86th, 130th, 20th, and 55th largest industrial firms, respectively. The imbroglio was ignited when William Agee and Mary Cunningham, graduates of the Harvard Business School who carried on a well-publicized office romance while running Bendix, and whose picture would later appear on the cover of *People* magazine, launched a $1.5 billion takeover offer for Martin Marietta, the giant defense contractor. Martin Marietta resisted. It unveiled a $1.5 billion counteroffer bid to take over Bendix! It was a Pac-Man defense strategy described this way by one merger specialist: "That's where my client eats yours before yours eats mine." The two firms quickly became locked in a death grip in which each seemed simultaneously to own the other.

To break the logjam, United Technologies entered the fray on Martin Marietta's side and offered to shore up Martin Marietta's offer for Bendix. Now desperate, Bendix turned to yet a fourth firm—Allied Corporation—as a partner to aid its effort to swallow Martin Marietta. When the dust finally settled, Allied had gobbled up Bendix, while a side deal enabled Martin Marietta to buy back its corporate freedom. Agee was released as president of Bendix.

Agee and Cunningham married and rode off into the sunset together, their fall from grace considerably softened by Agee's $4.1 million golden parachute. Said finance professor Fred C. Yeager: "It puts me in mind of the phalarope syndrome—you know, the African bird that spends its entire life chasing its own tail." As Chrysler's Lee Iacocca saw it, the affair wasn't a merger at all; it was "a three-ring circus." Other words used to describe it were "burlesque," "farce," and "tragicomedy."[1]

But Allied's appetite for acquisitions had only been whetted. Three years later, in 1985, it acquired Signal Companies, a leading aerospace producer, and the nation's 61st largest industrial concern. Thus Allied, which initially had ranked 55th among the Fortune 500 at the beginning of the decade, had now moved up to 37th. In acquiring Bendix and Signal, Allied had picked up businesses generating combined sales of $10 billion.

Like Alice in Wonderland, the game got curiouser and curiouser. Nabisco and Standard Brands merged in 1981, in a $2 billion deal that combined the nation's 152nd and 128th largest manufacturers, and that consolidated Nabisco's familiar household products (Oreo and Fig Newton cookies, Ritz crackers, Shredded Wheat, Cream of Wheat, Milk Bone dog biscuits) with those of Standard Brands (Planter's nuts, Royal gelatin, Baby Ruth and Butterfinger candy bars, Benedictine liqueur, Inver House scotch whiskey). The resulting amalgam, Nabisco Brands, jumped to 54th on the Fortune 500 list.

But the game had just begun. In 1985, Nabisco Brands was acquired by R. J. Reynolds (the nation's 23rd largest industrial firm) in a $5 billion deal combining one of the country's biggest tobacco companies with one of the largest food producers. Then, in 1988, RJR-Nabisco became a corporate combat zone in a fierce buyout battle between F. Ross Johnson, the firm's president, and the leveraged-buyout firm of Kohlberg Kravis Roberts. Having ridden mergers to the top of RJR-Nabisco management, Johnson now concluded that the combination of tobacco and food products, over which he had presided, no longer made economic sense. Kohlberg Kravis, on the other hand, sought to protect what it considered its "franchise" as the nation's largest leveraged-buyout operator. Kohlberg Kravis won, in a record deal valued at $25 billion—a sum more than double the combined value of *all* U.S. corporate mergers and acquisitions in 1975! Mr. Johnson lost and his portrait adorned the cover of *Time* magazine—but a scathing article questioned the role of unbridled greed in corporate America.

In this Kafkaesque era, deals became mega-deals to join companies together and then to put them asunder. In 1983, Esmark, marketer of Swift meats, Butterball turkeys, Playtex products, and STP oil treatments, spent $1 billion to acquire Norton Simon, producer of Hunt's tomato products, Wesson oil, Reddi-wip, Orville Redenbacher's popcorn, Johnny Walker scotch, the Avis rental car service, and Max Factor cosmetics. The next year, Esmark–Norton Simon was acquired by Beatrice Foods, maker of La Choy, Rosarita, Tropicana fruit drinks, Jolly Rancher candies, Milk Duds, Airstream motor homes, Samsonite luggage, Stiffel lamps, and Culligan water softeners. Two years later, in 1986, Beatrice–Norton Simon–Esmark (which now ranked as the nation's 26th largest industrial concern) was bought out by Kohlberg Kravis Roberts in a $6.2 billion deal. And for what purpose? To sell off the various Beatrice–Esmark–Norton Simon divisions that had just been consolidated!

Consider Kraft. In 1980, Dart Industries (producer of Tupperware, West Bend appliances, and Duracell batteries) merged with Kraft. Over the next six years, Dart & Kraft bought 32 companies (for $1.2 billion) and sold 38 businesses (for $1.3 billion). But in 1986, Dart & Kraft turned its penchant for deal-making on itself. The constituent firms split again, and undid the merger of six years earlier. Two years later, in 1988, Kraft was acquired again, this time by Philip Morris, in what was then a record-breaking $13.4 billion deal. Philip Morris, which had acquired General Foods in 1985, now became one of the ten largest American manufacturing firms. Combined under its corporate roof were Marlboro cigarettes, Miller beer, Jell-O gelatin, Post cereals, Kool-Aid, Maxwell House coffee, Oscar Meyer meats, Miracle Whip, Velveeta, Lender's bagels, Seven Seas salad dressings, Sealtest dairy products, and Breyer's ice cream.

The game continued, as if no one could resist the siren call. In the early 1980s General Motors was being thrashed by innovative, fuel-efficient, foreign-produced automobiles, particularly from Japan. GM's per-car costs were rising steadily to become the highest (and the worst) in the industry; its market share was falling. In 1980 it suffered a financial loss of $1.6 billion—its first annual corporate loss since the 1920s. But despite record plant closings and job layoffs, GM shelled out $2.6 billion in 1984 to acquire Electronic Data Systems (EDS), and another $4.7 billion in 1985 to buy the giant defense contractor Hughes Aircraft. The EDS acquisition was motivated in important part by GM chairman Roger Smith's desire to inject EDS founder H. Ross Perot's freewheeling—and highly successful—entrepreneurship into the smug, stodgy GM bureaucracy. This kind of new blood on the firm's board of directors, Smith thought, was just the tonic GM needed. In fact, he joked that Perot had his personal permission to shoot on sight the first GM bureaucrat who showed up at EDS toting a GM procedures manual.

And Perot didn't waste time or mince words. "We've got to nuke the GM system," he suggested as an essential first step. Next would be eliminating waste in the form of executive perks: "This includes items such as chauffeured limousines, heated garages, multitiered layers of executive dining rooms, and a vast array of other relics from the past that have nothing to do with building the best cars in the world." Executive attitudes would be next: "Okay, guys, I'm going to give you the whole code on what's wrong. You don't like your customers. You don't like your dealers. You don't like the people who make your cars. You don't like your stockholders. And, to a large extent, you don't like one another." And he attacked bonuses paid to top executives at the same time that workers were being laid off, saying "it's as though the generals at Valley Forge had bought new uniforms for themselves, when the troops were fighting in the snow barefooted."

Roger Smith soon decided that this was more entrepreneurship than he had bargained for. He now announced another deal: In mid-1986, he offered to pay Perot $700 million in order to buy him out of GM, remove him from the firm, and extract from him a promise that he would cease his criticism of GM. Although he accepted the deal, Perot did so with a withering parting shot: "At a time when GM is closing nine plants, putting over 30,000 people out of work, cutting back on capital expenditures, losing market share and having problems with profitability, is paying me $700 million the highest and best use of GM's capital? That amount of money will buy you a brand spanking new car plant and the jobs that go with it."

Consolidations fusing together competitors in the same industry or the same market were especially pronounced during the decade. These *horizontal* mergers, which concentrate industry control into fewer hands and undermine competition by reducing the number of competitors, proceeded at a pace, and on a scale, not seen since the epic turn-of-the-century merger, trust, and monopolization movement that created such giants as Standard Oil, American Tobacco, U.S. Steel, International Harvester, and General Electric.

In the oil industry, for example, Occidental Petroleum (12th largest oil firm) acquired Cities Service (19th largest oil company). Chevron (5th largest oil firm) acquired Gulf (6th largest oil company) in a record-breaking $13.3 billion deal. Texaco (3rd largest oil company) *thought* it had acquired Getty Oil (13th largest oil firm) in a $10.1 billion deal. (When a jury later concluded that Texaco had illegally interfered with Pennzoil's agreement to acquire Getty, a $10 billion judgment against Texaco forced the firm to declare bankruptcy.) Also notable were the 1984 merger between Mobil Oil, the 2nd largest integrated oil company, and Superior Oil, the nation's largest independent explorer and producer of oil and natural gas; and Occidental's $2.6 billion acquisition of Midcon, one of the nation's largest gas pipelines.

As of 1984, six of the eight largest corporate mergers in American industrial history involved oil companies, a combined aggregate expenditure totaling $45 billion. These mega-consolidations were disturbing in a variety of ways. As Ohio Senator Howard Metzenbaum pointed out, they were occurring at the same time that the oil companies were lobbying Congress for all sorts of favors and privileges—ostensibly, they said, in order to increase domestic oil reserves and production, and to lessen America's dependence on foreign supplies. " 'Preserve the oil depletion,' [the oil companies] said, 'and we will have more money for exploration.' So Congress did. 'Preserve the intangible drilling deduction, and we will have more money for drilling.' So Congress did. 'Give us oil price decontrols and we will have more money for exploration.' So Congress did. 'Give us special tax breaks for synthetic fuels development.' So Congress did. 'Roll back the windfall profits tax.' So Congress did that, too."[2] But instead of finding *new* oil deposits, developing *new* reserves, or producing *new* supplies of crude oil, Big Oil was merely shifting ownership of existing deposits, reserves, and supplies, and consolidating an already concentrated industry. Republican Congressman Silvio Conte mused that when the oil merger wave crested, "the only thing getting drilled will be the American people, and the only thing being pumped will be huge profits from the pockets of consumers."[3]

In food production and grocery retailing, horizontal consolidations proceeded at an equally torrid pace. General Foods, for example, acquired Oscar Mayer meats in 1981, and Entenman's bakery products in 1982. Then, in 1985, General Foods (including Oscar Mayer and Entenman's) was bought by Philip Morris, in a $5.6 billion acquisition. Three years later, Philip Morris acquired Kraft foods, combining it with General Foods. ConAgra, a privately held concern, purchased a controlling interest in Swift meats and Armour foods; bought Monfort, one of the nation's largest cattle feeding operations; acquired E. A. Miller, another large feedlot operator; bought Peavey, one of the nation's largest flour millers; and, in late 1988, competed with poultry giant Tyson to acquire Holly Farms, a leading producer of packaged poultry. Demure Sara Lee Corp. diversified into hog butchering by buying a number of regional sausage producers, including Kahns, Jimmy Dean, Hillshire Farms, and Bryans. As a result of these consolidations, according to agricultural economist Bruce W. Marion, American meatpacking has rapidly become a shared monopoly, in which the three largest meatpackers now collectively control 60 percent of the business nationwide—a level of industry control exceeding that which existed in 1920, when the Justice Department attacked the market power wielded by the Big Four packers.

In grocery retailing, horizontal consolidations between competitors have matched those on the food production side of the market. Between 1980 and 1987, more than 100 mergers and acquisitions worth $25 billion ($7.5 billion in 1987 alone) were consummated between grocery retailers. According to industry analyst Ronald Cotterill, the ten largest chains accounted for 87 percent of all grocery store acquisitions in 1986, and 63 percent in 1987. Cotterill estimates that by lessening competition, these mergers will raise food prices to consumers in 16 metropolitan areas across the country by a half-billion dollars per year.

Department store retailing has also been the scene of furious consolidations between competitors, primarily due to the agglomerative instincts of a single person. As recently as October 1986, Robert Campeau was an obscure Canadian real estate developer. The son of a French Catholic auto mechanic, Campeau got his first job at 15 using his deceased brother's baptismal certificate to prove he was old enough to sweep floors at a nickel smelting plant. Ten years later, he moved into real estate development after discovering that he could sell the house he was building for his family for an immediate $2,300 profit. He quit his smelting job and became a full-time builder. He pushed his development business to the limit, forcing Ottawa to abandon its height restrictions on high-rise buildings, and lobbying Toronto to adjust its zoning laws and approve a planned 68-story skyscraper.

But rebuffed by Canada's capital market, in what he considered to be anti-French bigotry, Campeau turned his sights on the American market. In two years, and with two multibillion-dollar deals, he became the largest department store operator in the United States. In 1986, Campeau launched a successful $3.6 billion takeover raid on Allied Stores that gave him control of 22 department store chains, including Jordan Marsh, Stern's, Maas Brothers, Ann Taylor, Brooks Brothers, Bonwit Teller, and Garfinckel's.

Two years later, in 1988, Campeau launched a takeover offer for Federated Department Stores, whose holdings included Bloomingdale's, Filene's, Burdine's, Lazarus, Bullocks, I. Magnin, Rich's, and Gold Circle. This time, Campeau precipitated a knock-down dragout battle. Federated wriggled desperately to remain free, filing lawsuits challenging the offer and rejecting Campeau's steadily rising bids. Then, in a surprise move, retailing giant R. H. Macy & Co. burst on the scene, joined in the battle for Federated, and topped Campeau's highest offer by nearly a half-billion dollars. As the bids and counterbids shot through the roof, Campeau and Macy declared a truce. For $6.6 billion, Campeau would gain control of Federated, while agreeing to sell two of Federated's chains to Macy.

Robert Campeau had not only become—almost overnight—the largest department store retailer in the country; he now was a kingpin in mall development, because he controlled a vast stable of the kinds of major department stores needed to "anchor" successful malls. As the *Wall Street Journal* reported, Campeau understood well that "if someone owned both the mall and the retailer, he could eliminate a lot of competition."[4]

The video entertainment field—movie production and distribution, theaters, cable television, cable programming, broadcasting—was also the scene of a furious consolidation movement. Since the mid-1980s, the major movie companies have acquired 14 theater chains (representing some 4,000 screens across the country), and have come to control important first-run theaters in major metropolitan areas like New York City and Chicago. The movie giants have also acquired local broadcast television stations and cable and pay television operations. The movie giants, says Barry Diller, chief executive officer of Twentieth Century–Fox, are "absolutely driven and committed to seeing that all these further possibilities offered by the new technologies are not going to be exploited without [the giants] being able to exercise their historical leverage."[5]

Cable television companies too have rushed to merge with one another. In 1987 alone, some $7 billion of cable television properties were consolidated. John C. Malone has spent $3 billion acquiring control of 150 local cable television systems since 1980, as well as acquiring a dominant financial interest in Ted Turner's cable programming operations. Malone's company, Tele-Communications Inc., is now the country's largest cable television operator, and Malone is called "the king of cable TV." Says one broker, Malone is "a sort of Godfather of the industry. Everybody owes something to John."[6]

In early 1989, a veritable blockbuster of a consolidation was announced between Time, Inc. (which owns HBO, the nation's largest movie programming service for cable TV, and which also operates the nation's second largest chain of local cable TV systems) and Warner Communications, a leading producer of movies and television programs, as well as the nation's fifth largest local cable TV system operator.

Shortly thereafter, Paramount (formerly Gulf & Western) entered the fray with a spectacular $10.7 billion hostile tender offer for Time, making it a three-cornered bidding contest for prime media properties.[7] Commenting on this affair, Robert Hughes, a senior writer at *Time*, dubbed the takeover battle as "another disaster of late capitalism, with all these plastic dinosaurs bashing against one another in the primeval swamp. I don't have any faith in the ability of people whose business it is to sell each other the rights to videotapes and junk bonds to run great publishing houses to everybody's benefit. I am still old-fashioned enough to think of Time as a publishing house."[8]

And the list of anticompetitive industry consolidations goes on—from airlines, home appliances, and paper products, to textiles, apparel, and steel.

The game was not limited to American players. Corporate dealmania went global during the decade, as American and foreign competitors rushed to merge with one another. Japanese tiremaker Bridgestone bought Firestone. The British firm Tate & Lyle acquired Staley Continental (a leading U.S. producer of corn sweeteners) and Amstar (the largest U.S. refiner of cane sugar, operating under the Domino label). Swiss food giant Nestlé bought Carnation Foods. Other industries in which U.S. firms merged with major foreign rivals include electrical power generating equipment, industrial gases, paints, chemicals, home appliances, agricultural feed products, glass, and wines and spirits.[9]

At the same time, but not included in the merger statistics, a raft of "quasi-consolidations," or "joint ventures," has organizationally linked the American automobile oligopoly with its foreign rivals. These joint ventures include: GM/Toyota, GM/Daewoo, GM/Suzuki, GM/Isuzu, GM/Lotus, Ford/Mazda, Ford/Mazda/Kia, Ford/Volkswagen, Chrysler/Mitsubishi, Chrysler/Mitsubishi/Hyundai, Chrysler/Samsung, Chrysler/Fiat, and Chrysler/Maserati. Similar joint venture deals have proliferated between Japanese and American producers of steel. Overwhelmed by this vast intercorporate web of cross-ownership, joint production, and co-supply arrangements, an exasperated Congressman from Illinois, Richard Durbin, exclaimed: "It used to be 'us' versus 'them.' Now, we don't know who's 'us' and who's 'them.' "[10]

The upshot, according to calculations by Martin and Susan Tolchin, is that "foreign investors own close to $445 billion in U.S. bank assets, more than $300 billion in diversified stocks and bonds, more than $100 billion in real estate, and $200–$300 billion in direct investments in factories, warehouses, and assembly plants." Japanese companies now own more than 600 American factories and employ more than 200,000 American workers.

For specific U.S. industries, *Fortune* estimates the degree of foreign ownership as follows: Chemicals (more than 30 percent foreign-owned); glass, stone, and clay products (more than 20 percent); primary metals (20 percent); printing and publishing (more than 10 percent); electrical machinery (more than 10 percent); and food (approximately 10 percent). As one result, the Tolchins point out, decisions "that used to be made in Sacramento, Albany, and Washington D.C., are now being made in Tokyo, London, and Riyadh."[11]

Other trends were notable during the decade. Divestitures and spin-offs of operations swelled along with corporate consolidations. In 1987, 1,119 deals worth an estimated $52.2 billion involved divestitures of operations.

Leveraged buyouts—where control of corporate operations is bought from public stockholders, and the firms are "taken private"—exploded 700 percent in value during the decade, from $4.5 billion in 1983 to $35.6 billion by 1987.[12] ("Leverage" here simply means the use of debt to finance an acquisition, and pledging the acquired company's assets as collateral for the loans.)

Junk bonds—low-grade, high-risk bonds traditionally used by small firms desperately in need of capital funds for expansion, but lacking a reliable financial track record—were turned into volatile fuel for the deal-making fire. Issues of junk bonds escalated to nearly $30 billion by 1987, and they have come to play a critical role in financing corporate deal-mania. According to calculations by Barrie Wigmore, partner in the Goldman Sachs investment bank, the fraction of junk bonds issued for purposes of mergers and acquisitions shot up from 6 percent in 1982 to nearly 80 percent by 1987.[13]

Driven by deal-mania, corporate debt exploded. While manufacturers' profits after taxes fluctuated up and down around the $90 billion mark, corporate debt in the manufacturing sector rose 72 percent, from $292 billion in 1980 to $501 billion by 1986.[14] The burden of paying the interest on this expanding debt load has grown too. According to economist Benjamin M. Friedman, during the fifties and sixties, interest payments on average claimed only 16 percent of corporate earnings. In the seventies, that amount was up to 33 percent. "But by 1986," Friedman points out, "American business corporations needed 56 percent of available earnings just to pay interest."[15]

A fierce new species burst on the scene—the corporate raider. T. Boone Pickens (the friend of "Joe Six Pack"), Carl Icahn (the stockholder's "Robin Hood"), Irwin Jacobs ("Irv the Liquidator"), Asher Edelman, Sir James Goldsmith, and Saul Steinberg tapped vast reservoirs of funds to finance hostile raids. Their two-tiered, front-end-loaded, bootstrap, bust-up raids struck fear in the hearts of incumbent managements. With the raiders able to mount multibillion-dollar threats to take over such giants as Phillips Petroleum, Gulf Oil, TWA, and Goodyear Tire & Rubber, no firm—no matter how big—seemed safe.

The score on another front was also impressive: Crime in the suites became a commonplace. Guilty pleas to felony charges of insider trading and securities fraud, prison sentences, and criminal fines and penalties have expanded in step with corporate deal-mania. Ivan Boesky extolled the virtues of greed and the wonders of stock arbitrage—and was fined $100 million and shipped off to federal prison for criminal trading on insider information. Dennis Levine, Marty Siegel, and the Yuppie Four pleaded guilty to similar charges.

After being acquired by General Electric, the investment bank Kidder Peabody paid more than $20 million to settle criminal charges of insider trading. And in late 1988, Drexel Burnham—the pioneer and king of junk bond financing for corporate deals—pleaded guilty to six felony charges and agreed to pay a record fine of $650 million. "In the highest of high finance," John Kenneth Galbraith admonishes, "the paths of presumed financial intelligence lead regularly, if not to the grave, at least to minimum security slammers."[16]

In one way or another, the scandal on Wall Street has been closely connected with corporate mergers, acquisitions, and deals. In fact, the growing flood of confessions and indictments suggests that these were not merely isolated transgressions; instead, they appeared to be an integral part of the game. Observes Ira Lee Sorkin, former head of the Securities and Exchange Commission's New York office, about the scandal on Wall Street: "When this thing moved to Boesky, the whole manner of the investigation changed. It was no longer a guy buying or selling information. It was focused on the ways that Wall Street tried to get the deals done. Insider trading was just part of the scheme."[17]

Meanwhile the Reagan administration, by declining to enforce the antitrust laws, allowed the game to proliferate and expand. The Justice Department challenged a minuscule number (twenty-six) of the nearly 11,000 corporate deals for which premerger notification was required (Table 3). Indeed, ardent Reaganauts relaxed merger policy with their merger "guidelines" of 1982 and again with the "revised" guidelines of 1984. In 1986, the administration asked Congress to gut the nation's antimerger law by new legislation. Commerce Secretary Malcolm Baldrige went even further. He urged that the merger law be abolished outright—a position some prominent neoliberals supported. The Reagan administration slashed the number of attorneys in the Justice Department's Antitrust Division by 44 percent, and cut the agency's full-time staff (including economists, paralegals, and clerical-secretarial support) by 37 percent. The "stark truth," according to Donald Baker, an-

TABLE 3

MERGER POLICY UNDER THE REAGAN ADMINISTRATION

	Justice Department		Federal Trade Commission	
Year	Premerger Notifications Received	Cases Filed	Premerger Notifications Received	Administrative Complaints Filed
1981	993	3	996	6
1982	1,204	3	1,203	2
1983	1,101	2	1,093	1
1984	1,339	5	1,340	3
1985	1,604	5	1,603	2
1986	1,949	4	1,949	3
1987	2,533	4	1,346	0
TOTAL	10,723	26	9,530	17

Source: Trial Lawyers for Public Justice, Washington, D.C., November 22, 1988.

titrust chief in the Ford administration, "is that the Antitrust Division today is less than two-thirds its size when President Reagan took office. It is smaller than when I came to it first in October 1966. . . ."[18]

And so the merger game goes on. On a good day, it's like Alice in Wonderland. On a bad day, it's like Life in Kafkaland.

Why is this bizarre game played?

Who are the players?

Who are the winners? Who are the losers?

Most important, does the game itself make any sense?

Let's look at the scorecard.

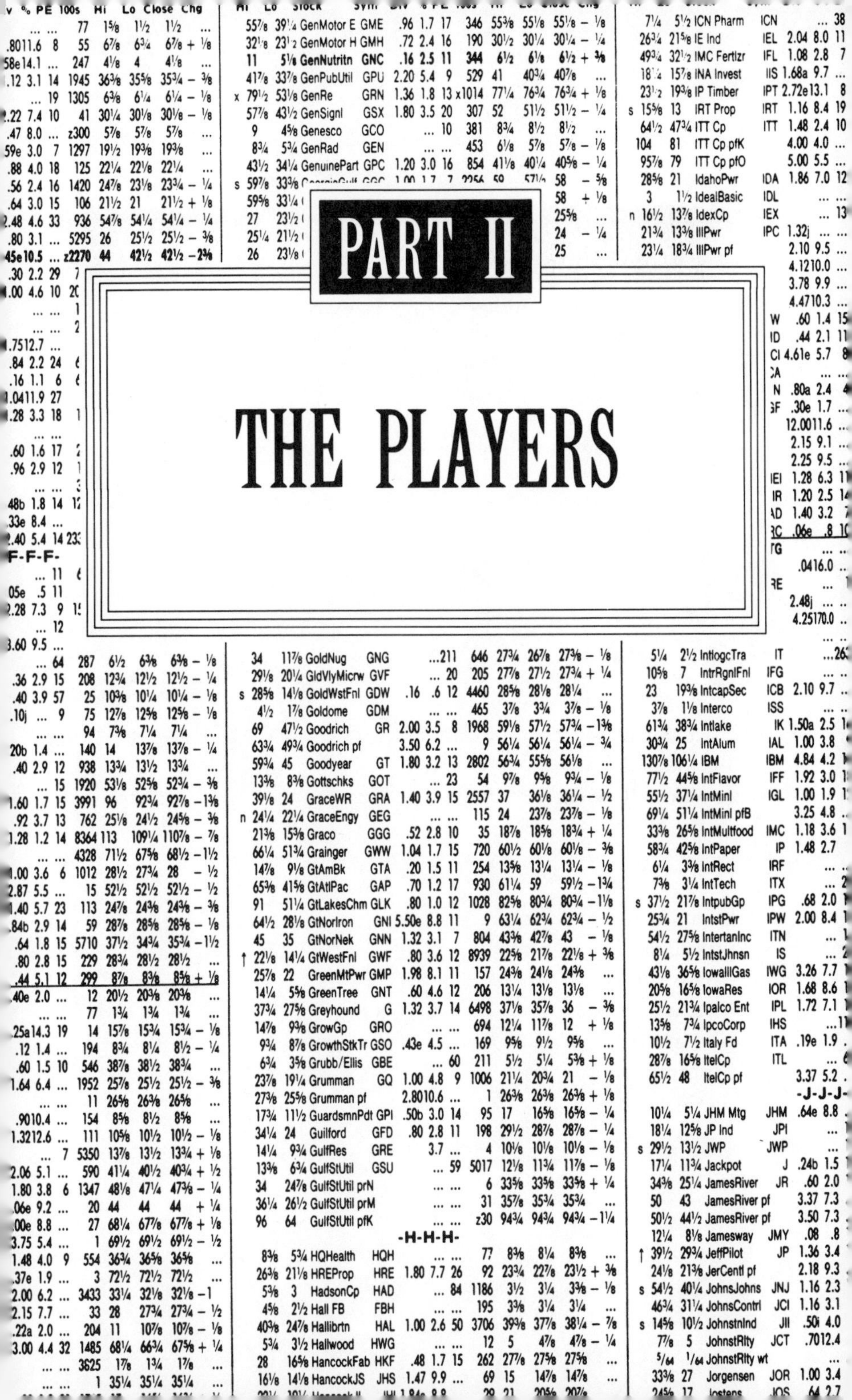

PART II

THE PLAYERS

3

THE OUTSIDE RAIDERS

I'm sick of people calling me a corporate gunslinger.
—T. Boone Pickens

To some, they are predators, piranhas, greenmailers. To others, they are the necessary catalysts for shaking up stodgy managements and for restoring giant corporations to their owners, the shareholders. Alan Greenspan, chairman of the Federal Reserve, calls them (in dispassionate bureaucratese) "unaffiliated corporate restructurers" who strike when they see "suboptimal asset allocation." They are the raiders—a flamboyant coterie of takeover artists playing leading roles in a convoluted Wall Street drama.

Carl Icahn, the Princeton-trained, shrewdly analytical, battle-scarred veteran of raids against such formidable redoubts as Texaco, TWA, and USX, seems to love to be hated. According to one raider, Icahn's favorite quote is "If you want a friend, buy a dog." Nevertheless, he describes himself as a corporate Robin Hood. His mission, as he sees it, is to "stop oppression of shareholders" by American management. He believes hostile takeovers are the means to that end: "The takeover boom is a treatment for a disease that is destroying American productivity: gross and widespread incompetent management. Takeovers are part of a free-market response, working to unseat corporate bureaucracies, control runaway costs and make America competitive again."

"Top management in this country is mediocre," says Icahn, "yet we do very little about it. Corporate executives are judged by their peers not on how profitable their departments are, but on how many people report to them. The chief executive officer's compensation is often based on the size of the company rather than the company's profitability."

"American CEOs, while not the best and the brightest," he claims, "generally select seconds-in-command who are not quite as bright as they are" because "smarter ones would constitute a threat." Then, when the CEO retires, that second-in-command takes the reins, thus insuring "the survival of the unfittest." At the same time, many companies "are burdened by layers of vice presidents who not only don't produce, but are often counter-productive." This transforms the executive suite into a "corporate welfare state." Given the lack of accountability in corporate democracy, Icahn concludes, "the most effective way to remove ineffective management and enhance productivity is through a takeover and/or a leveraged buyout. . . . If we do nothing to redeem our corporations, future historians will marvel at why, when we could have so easily. However, it is still not too late, and takeovers are an essential part of the solution."[1]

There are many of these flamboyant raiders. One is William F. Farley, veteran of three failed marriages and numerous amorous escapades without benefit of clergy.[2] The son of a mailman, Farley attended Catholic schools, developed a passion for sports, and earned a scholarship to Bowdoin College in Maine. After finishing college and going on to earn a law degree, Farley moved into—and out of—a number of corporate positions. He was frustrated. He hungered to make his own deals, rather than to assist at the deals instigated by others.

By 1976, Farley had had enough. He struck out to acquire companies and to implement corporate deals of his own devising. In his first acquisition, he bought a citrus processing firm for $1.7

million. He put down only $25,000 of his own money, and borrowed the remainder. Over the next few years, he replicated this kind of highly leveraged deal on an ever-escalating scale. In 1985, with junk bond financing provided by Drexel Burnham, Farley bought Northwest Industries—a sprawling conglomerate whose most prominent division included Fruit of the Loom underwear and Acme boots—for $1.4 billion. Farley dismembered Northwest, using part of the proceeds to pay down some of the debt from his prior deals and part to pay himself. The remainder was devoted to his acquisition fund to finance future corporate purchases.

Farley's debt load was ballooning—and so was his lifestyle: an apartment on Chicago's Gold Coast, houses in Colorado and Maine, a boat in Florida, a California vineyard, and a minority stake in the Chicago White Sox. Farley's biggest and most bitterly contested raid came in 1988, when he trained his sights on West Point–Pepperell, the nation's largest textile and apparel producer. Pepperell management vowed to resist the depredations of this Yankee carpetbagger. "We are going to fight Farley until hell freezes over," vowed Pepperell president Joseph Lanier, a Harvard-educated Southerner who had spent his entire career with his family's company. "And then we are going to fight him on the ice." Georgia's governor and many of the state's legislators joined in the battle to defeat Farley's raid on Pepperell.

In the end, Farley prevailed. In early 1989, he won control of West Point–Pepperell for $3 billion. Like his other acquisitions, this one would be highly leveraged. "God forbid we have a recession or interest rates begin to rise," worried one financial analyst at the time of the deal. "This is not one of those deals where he can make a single mistake." For his part, the 46-year-old Farley dismissed their concerns. "Bill Farley knows only one pace," he said of himself, "and that's a fast pace." He had been living with high, growing debt loads for a decade. "Why worry now?" he said.

The quintessential raider, however, is T. Boone Pickens. Trained as a petroleum geologist, he founded Mesa Petroleum and built it into the largest "independent" in the Texas oil patch. A maverick by predisposition, with an instinctive feel for the dynamics of the oil industry, Pickens made a remarkable discovery: In the late 1970s, with industrywide "finding costs" of oil at $15 a barrel, it was cheaper to prospect on the floor of the New York Stock Exchange than in the jungles of Indonesia or the icy slopes of Alaska. Pickens calculated that if he could take over a major oil company—say Cities Service, Phillips, Gulf, or Unocal—he could acquire oil reserves at the bargain basement prices of $5 a barrel. This made sense as a straight business proposition, but it would require a knockdown–drag-out battle against the oil establishment.

Pickens knew that the crusade, if it was to be successful, could not be fought for such mundane goals as self-enrichment or self-aggrandizement. It had to be embellished with altruistic ideals and clothed in a noble public purpose. David had to take on Goliath as the protagonist for all the little people. "I am out there working for Joe Sixpack," he was fond of telling bemused reporters. (His detractors call him the "Attila from Amarilla.")

Pickens (and his fellow raiders) embraced a populist theme. "We want to establish one thing," he said, "and that is that stockholders own companies, and management are employees."[3] That means facing up to one of the basic problems in America today—the separation of ownership and control. Believe it or not, says Pickens, 9 percent of the CEOs from the Fortune 500 don't own a single share of stock in the companies they run, yet they have absolute control over assets worth billions of dollars. Few of these "good ol' boys" have ever made money on their own. They are bureaucrats and caretakers, not entrepreneurs. They have climbed the corporate ladder with a minimum of risk. By the time they reach the top, they are no longer in touch with reality. Like other bureaucrats, their main concern is with executive perks, bigger budgets, and expanding empires. They have little interest in serving the stockholders who own the companies that employ them.

The professional managers, endowed with "tenure" and insulated from accountability to stockholders, have not delivered the goods. "It's unusual to find a large corporation that's efficient," says Pickens. "I know about economies of scale and all the other advantages that are supposed to come with size. But when you get an inside look, it's easy to see how inefficient big business really is. . . . If we encouraged the breakup of some of the inefficient ones and allowed some of their divisions to start anew, America would be astounded at the results."[4]

The performance of the major oil companies provides ample evidence to support Pickens's allegations. After the meteoric rise of oil prices during the boom years of the 1970s, the majors were awash in cash flow. (In many cases profits and cash flow doubled and trebled in the space of a year.) But this windfall was squandered on some of the most infelicitious ventures in the history of corporate America. Like a rich kid in a toy store, Big Oil bought everything in sight.

The rationale was "diversification." Someday, oil reserves would be depleted and the companies did not want to be left holding an empty bag. So, Exxon acquired Reliance Electric for $1.2 billion (twice the company's market value); Mobil bought Montgomery Ward for $1.5 billion (an acquisition *Forbes* called "Mobil's Monkey"); Atlantic Richfield bought Anaconda Copper for $2.1 billion; Sohio bought Kennecott Copper for $1.8 billion; Texaco bought Getty (and with it ESPN and Madison Square Garden), and Gulf was rumored to be contemplating the purchase of the New York Knickerbockers and Ringling Bros., Barnum & Bailey Circus. By the 1980s, these acquisitions had turned to dross. Oil companies, it seemed, were not particularly adept at running copper mines, mail-order houses, financial institutions, and television networks. Most of the acquired properties were therefore divested, with the oil companies incurring sizable writeoffs on their profit-and-loss statements.

The epitaph on this diversification strategy appeared in a *Fortune* article on April 30, 1984, entitled "The Decade's Worst Mergers." Four of the seven involved the country's largest oil companies: Exxon, Mobil, Sohio, and Atlantic Richfield. In 1983, according to

Fortune's estimates, the losses at Reliance dragged down Exxon's per-share earnings by 6 percent; only its huge size saved Exxon from greater suffering. Mobil's earnings were 39 percent lower than they would have been if Mobil had eschewed shopping malls and stuck to the oil patch. Had Atlantic Richfield stayed out of the copper pits, its earnings per share would have been almost 25 percent higher. Kennecott's losses cost Sohio even more—$1.87 a share on earnings of $6.14. Collectively, these companies had plowed hundreds of millions of dollars into their besieged acquisitions (on top of the purchase prices), but none of them produced a penny of profit. Indeed, the oil giants could have significantly bolstered both their earnings and the price of their stock if, instead of making these conglomerate acquisitions, they had invested the purchase prices in the stock of their own companies.

Such instances of poor management did not escape the attention of the raiders prowling the oil patch. But there were other lures. Oil prices, although off their 1979 peaks, were still high and generating massive cash flows for the majors. Oil stocks on Wall Street were selling at substantial discounts from their book value, and the "breakup" value of the integrated majors exceeded—at times, by a substantial margin—the putative price that would have to be paid to acquire the companies. Finally, the advent of the Reagan administration made a serious antitrust challenge to mergers, takeovers, and acquisitions an unlikely probability. The plums seemed ripe for the picking.

Pickens made a modest start. His first run was at Supron Energy, a medium-sized oil and gas company. In the ensuing bidding war, the company was acquired by someone else. But Pickens made a net profit of more than $22 million from the increase in the price of Supron's stock.

His next target was Cities Service (1982), an integrated oil company more than twenty times the size of his Mesa Petroleum. Again Mesa lost out in the bidding war—this time to Occidental—but Pickens ended up with a profit of $44 million on an investment of

$182 million. His net after expenses and taxes was $13 million for holding Cities Service stock less than six months.

Next came General American Oil Company in December 1982. GAO's stock had traded for as little as $24 a share as recently as the summer of 1982. Pickens offered $40. Again there was a bidding war, and again Pickens lost. Again a white knight took over the target company. On January 10, 1983, Phillips announced that it would buy all of GAO's outstanding stock at $45 a share. Mesa's profit for "failing" to acquire was a net of $25.3 million on an investment of roughly $32 million for a period of little more than one month.

After a brief play in Superior Oil (which netted a profit of $31.6 million), Pickens was prepared for the big time. He set his sights of Gulf, the 6th largest oil company and the 11th largest industrial corporation in the United States. Gulf was 75 times bigger than Mesa Petroleum. It would take more than a powerful trumpet to make its walls crumble; in fact, it eventually took $13.2 billion.

As Pickens saw it, Gulf was ripe for a raider. In 1975, it lost its drilling concessions in Kuwait and Venezuela. In 1976, its board chairman had to resign in the wake of a political scandal. It was accused of participating in a cartel that had artificially raised uranium prices. Its domestic oil reserves between 1975 and 1982 had dropped more than 40 percent, and its foreign reserves had declined even more. Most incriminating from Pickens' persepective, however, was that Gulf stock was selling for some $40 a share when its potential value, based on an appraisal of the company's assets, was $114.

Pickens launched his raid (with the help of a consortium) in October 1983. Gulf shares at the time sold for $41. By the time all the bids and counterbids had been tallied, Gulf had been sold to Chevron (Standard Oil of California) in March 1984 for $80 a share. Mesa and its partners had made $760 million in five months.

After the Gulf "victory," Pickens's raid on Phillips Petroleum was almost anticlimactic. Phillips was the nation's 10th largest oil company, with a billion dollars in cash in its treasury, and an estimated breakup value of between $70 and $80 a share if the company's constituent parts were sold off piecemeal on the open market. Unfortunately for Phillips, its very good health made it vulnerable: In September 1984, its stock was selling for only a little over $40 a share—approximately half the company's breakup value. Pickens moved in, triggering a bidding contest involving such heavy hitters as Carl Icahn, Irwin L. Jacobs, and Ivan Boesky. Again Pickens "lost"; Phillips succeeded in preserving its independence (perhaps at an exorbitant cost). Pickens's consolation: an $89 million pretax profit, plus $25 million for expenses—booty from a battle that lasted from December 1984 to March 1985.

What was the upshot of the financial razzle-dazzle in these deals? Who were the winners and losers? Was Pickens the primary beneficiary (to the tune of some $900 million) for his skill in putting target companies into play and then "outfumbling" rival bidders in acquiring them? Pickens, of course, vehemently denies that his raids are designed not to take over target companies, but to extort greenmail for leaving them to a white knight or to the incumbent management. Time and time again he tells anybody willing to listen:

> [Too many] managements say: "We're under terrible pressure. The raiders are after us, so we've got to perform on a short-term basis." The only reason the raiders are after them is because they've done such a lousy job, and the price of their stock is at a discount. The media and the investing public and the consumers of this country should be suspicious of some of these managements and say: "What are you talking about, short term, long term? What the hell have you guys been doing for the last 10 years?"[5]

In his appearance before the House Ways and Means Committee in April 1985, Pickens took pains to persuade Congress that the primary beneficiaries of his raids were the stockholders of the target companies whose share prices were undervalued by the market. He presented the information in Table 4 to show that—thanks to his raids against Cities Service, General American, Gulf, and Phillips, —770,000 shareholders had achieved a capital gain of $11.75 billion, while the federal government presumably collected an additional $3.5 billion in taxes. In another tabulation (Table 5), Pickens sought to demonstrate the gap between the appraised value of major oil companies and the price of their stock on Wall Street. Based on this calculation, Pickens told the committee that if these ten companies could bring the price of their stock up to just 75 percent of the companies' appraised value, some 4 million stockholders would enjoy a $75 billion bonanza. Takeovers, acquisitions, mergers, and leveraged buyouts, said Pickens, are simply efficient means to such worthy ends.

In somewhat more restrained rhetoric, the Council of Economic Advisers, with its staff of Chicago School, laissez-faire savants, endorses this policy. The success of the American economy, it claims, depends on competition not only in the market for goods and services, but also in the market for corporate control. Competition breaks down entrenched market positions, unsettles comfortable managerial lives, and provides incentives for innovative forms of business organization and finance.

However, the CEA points out, there is a flaw in the system: since corporations are generally owned by stockholders who delegate substantial decision-making authority to a group of hired managers; since these managers are primarily responsible for the corporation's success or failure; and since they typically own a relatively small percentage of the firm's shares, it is possible that management will operate the corporation in management's best interests, and not in the best interests of the corporation's stockholders. Therefore, says the council, corporate takeovers, and the raiders who generate them, serve a useful function. They are the principal corrective for this divergence in interest between managements and stockholders. They play a vital role in increasing national wealth. They improve efficiency, transfer scarce resources to better uses, and stimulate

TABLE 4

ANALYSIS OF SELECTED MERGERS

	Premerger Price per Share	Stock Price Alltime High (year)	Price per Share Achieved	Percentage Increase over Premerger Price	Number of Shareholders	Gain to Shareholders ($ millions)	Estimated Federal Income Taxes ($ millions)
Cities Service	$30	$68 (1981)	$52	73	150,000	$ 2,000	$ 600
General American Oil	30	57 (1980)	45	50	20,000	375	110
Gulf	40	54 (1980)	80	100	400,000	6,600	2,000
Phillips	35	63 (1980)	53	51	200,000	2,775	830
TOTALS					770,000	$11,750	$3,540

TABLE 5

VALUE VS. STOCK PRICE: MAJOR OIL COMPANIES

	Shares (millions)	Company Valuation* (per share)	March 12, 1985, Stock Price	Stock Price as Percent of Value	Appreciation to 75 percent ($ millions)
Chevron	342.1	$108.85	34.125	31.3	$16,255
Exxon	816.1	77.70	50.00	64.3	6,753
Mobil	411.4	88.35	30.00	33.9	14,918
Texaco	241.6	99.95	35.25	35.3	9,594
Arco	248.0	122.40	48.75	39.8	10,676
Amoco	270.3	108.45	62.75	57.6	5,024
Sohio	240.0	101.85	45.50	44.7	7,414
Sun	117.2	88.35	50.125	56.7	1,891
Unocal	173.7	76.45	46.875	61.3	1,817
Occidental	96.0	53.25	28.25	53.1	1,122
TOTAL					75,464

* by J. S. Herrold.

effective corporate management. They also help recapitalize firms so that their financial structures are more in line with prevailing market conditions. Most important—so this argument runs—they discipline managements and impose new corporate strategies in place of unsuccessful ones.[6]

Nevertheless, the deals by Icahn, Pickens, and other fabled buccaneers raise a number of fundamental questions.

Do they really benefit the small investor? Clearly, they do not enrich *all* stockholders of the target companies; the primary beneficiaries are those who were in on the two-tier offers. What about the stockholders of the acquiring companies? Their share values typically decline a year or two years after the deal is consummated. What about the bondholders in the surviving companies? Their securities are frequently downgraded because of the massive increase in the acquiring company's debt load and its deteriorating debt/equity ratio.

What happens if a raid is unsuccessful? The raider gets his greenmail—in effect, a fee for agreeing to desist from the proposed acquisition. But the target company has to pay a price for preserving its independence. The Phillips deal, as Eric Allison analyzed it,[7] poignantly illustrates why takeover raids can be so profitable and why critics of the raiders say their activities are destructive:

- Mesa and its partners made a profit of almost $90 million plus expenses.
- Icahn's syndicate got $75 million plus expenses.
- Drexel Burnham Lambert, Inc., got $14 million in fees.
- Morgan Stanley got at least $10 million for its services. (Had the restructuring plan gone through, it probably would have earned at least $35 million.)
- Phillips stayed independent, but the debentures it issued to buy up its stock left it with an $8 billion debt—80 percent of its total capital. Any dip in oil prices before sufficient assets were sold would make it difficult to pay the new dividend. It would have to sell $2 billion to $4 billion in assets to bring the debt down to a manageable level.
- The employees of Phillips, including those who lived in Bartlesville, faced job shifts due to the sale of the assets possibly more severe than if Pickens had taken over Phillips in the first place. Ten percent of its work force was offered early retirement in an effort to cut costs.
- Phillips CEO William C. Douce, whose purchase of Aminoil probably triggered the raid and who had seen his restructuring plan rejected by shareholders, announced his retirement.

Obviously, the bottom line on the raid was nothing to crow about.

If the raid is successful, the target company is typically broken up into its constituent parts. This is hardly the ideal method for restructuring corporate America. It raises fundamental questions about the acquisitions, mergers, and takeovers that put the target company together in the first place. It gives no assurance that yet another acquisition will prove to be the magic solution to the problem of excessive size, bureaucratic dry rot, managerial lethargy, and lackluster economic performance. When raiders tout the virtues of competition in the market for corporate control, are they not tacitly conceding the breakdown of competition in the market for goods and services? If competition functioned to discipline individual firms—as monopoly, oligopoly, and concentrated economic power do not—would takeovers be the preferred instrument for replacing mediocre managers with superior ones?

Finally, there is the question of company morale, up and down the line of the takeover target. The turmoil and confusion, the anxiety and apprehension that accompany a raid, whether it is successful or not, take their toll. Says *Fortune*:

> . . . the plant closings and headquarters shutdowns, the give-backs and two-tier wage scales imposed on production workers, the purges of middle managers that follow bust-ups, mergers, and slim-downs—all these stun not only victims but also survivors, suffusing them with insecurity. Every man for himself [is] the implicit message; if you don't look out for No. 1, you can bet no one else will. Certainly not the top guys in the company: spurred by their own fear of takeover, they often seem too busy protecting their own interests to attend to yours or the corporation's.[8]

"Restructuring," "redeployment of assets," "replacement of inferior managements" may be tantalizing slogans, and the raiders deserve credit for calling attention to the need for structural reform in giant corporations. However, this does not answer the question of whether corporate raiding is the right remedy, or whether it is merely another species of private profiteering without socially redeeming virtues.

4

THE INSIDE RAIDERS

They squeeze the orange
and throw away the skin.
—Voltaire,
Letter to Mme. Denis

Donald P. Kelly epitomizes the "inside" management raider. A legend in Chicago business circles, Kelly grew up on the city's tough South Side, and left home after high school to work construction jobs in Michigan and Texas. He served as a torpedoman in the Navy during World War II and admits that, at times, he was less than a model sailor. Thirty years later, after meeting Admiral Elmo Zumwalt, Kelly joked: "It was the first time I had ever met an admiral—other than at one of my court-martials."[1]

After the war, and with no college degree, Kelly joined Chicago meatpacker Swift & Co. He rose through the corporate ranks. In 1968, he became vice president for corporate development, where he led the effort to create Esmark, an umbrella company whose holdings later included Swift. Imbued with the then fashionable faith in the virtues of conglomerate diversification, Kelly turned Esmark into a deal-making machine. He embarked on a merger and acquisition campaign comprising the purchase (and sale) of some sixty businesses and operations. Prominent among these were

International Playtex, STP, Vickers Petroleum, and Mobil Oil's farm chemicals operations.

Each time he engineered a deal, Kelly had a plaque prominently affixed to the wall of his well-appointed office. He candidly admitted that in most of the fields he and Esmark had entered, his expertise was zero: "We've drilled holes in the ground in Ohio, sold meat in Madagascar, and produced bras in Puerto Rico," Kelly boasted. "All it tells you is that you can be head of a holding company and not be very smart about anything."[2]

In 1983, Kelly concluded his biggest corporate acquisition yet. In a $1 billion deal, he acquired Norton Simon, Inc., a giant conglomerate whose holdings included Hunt-Wesson foods, Max Factor cosmetics, and Avis rental cars. The following year, Kelly turned to inside raiding. He decided to cash in on the value of Esmark–Norton Simon. Aided by leveraged-buyout specialists Kohlberg Kravis Roberts, Kelly launched a $2.4 billion buyout bid to acquire Esmark–Norton Simon from its stockholders for $56 a share, and to take the firm private. But in an unanticipated development, Kelly's bid was thwarted. An outside buyer—Beatrice Foods—entered the game, and eventually succeeded in buying control of Kelly's firm for $60 a share, or $2.8 billion. Kelly was out. Although he personally benefitted from a golden parachute worth an estimated $18 million, Kelly seemed to have been defeated.

But appearances were deceiving. Two years later, in 1986, Kelly reentered the scene with a vengeance. Once again joining with Kohlberg Kravis Roberts, and with financing provided by Drexel Burnham's junk bonds, Kelly bought control of Beatrice—the firm that two years earlier had ousted him from Esmark—in a $6.2 billion buyout deal. The next year, Kelly elected to head E-II Holdings, a consumer products conglomerate spun off from Beatrice by Kohlberg Kravis Roberts. In 1988, Kelly sold E-II Holdings to American Brands for $1.1 billion. But the rumor was that an E-III Holdings was waiting in the wings.

TABLE 6

KKR'S MEGA BUYOUTS

Date	Acquisition	Purchase Price ($ billions)	Amount Borrowed ($ billions)
December 1988	RJR-Nabisco	$20.6	$18.6
October 1985	Beatrice	6.2	5.8
July 1986	Safeway Stores	4.1	3.7
December 1986	Owens-Illinois	3.7	3.5
July 1987	Jim Walter	2.4	2.3
April 1985	Storer Communications	2.4	2.2
April 1985	Union Texas Petroleum	2.2	2.0
June 1988	Duracell	1.8	1.5
June 1984	Pace Industries	1.6	1.4
March 1988	Stop & Shop	1.2	1.1
March 1984	Wometco	1.0	0.9

The Beatrice buyout in April 1986—the largest leveraged buyout on record up to that time—illustrates the mechanics of leveraged buyouts. Founded as a dairy concern in 1984 in Beatrice, Nebraska, the company had gone on a wild diversification spree that included acquisitions in such diverse fields as cosmetics, luggage, cold storage warehousing, Coca Cola bottling, and popcorn. At the time of the buyout, it was an ailing conglomerate with deplorable management.

Beatrice was bought by Kohlberg Kravis Roberts (KKR), Wall Street's No. 1 LBO boutique (see Table 6), headed by the dapper, polished Henry Kravis, art fancier and Manhattan socialite with a taste for high living. His name turns up frequently in gossip columns, and his pet causes include the Metropolitan Museum of Art and fundraising for the George Bush presidential campaign. Kravis makes hundreds of millions of dollars not by prospecting for oil, making steel, or inventing a better mousetrap. He doesn't spend a lifetime nurturing a business enterprise. His special skill consists of buying, selling, and repackaging enterprises built by others.

KKR bought Beatrice for $6.25 billion and in addition assumed the company's $1.7 billion debt, which brought the total cost of the buyout to $7.95 billion. KKR promptly installed Donald P. Kelly (the former Beatrice executive) as chief operating officer. To pay for the company, KKR raised a buyout fund (equity capital) of $1.35 billion, approximately half of which was supplied by pension funds and other institutional investors. The rest of the purchase price consisted of debt: $4 billion in bank loans and $2.5 billion in high-yield, low-value junk bonds marketed by the investment banking firm of Drexel Burnham Lambert.

The financial rewards of the deal were distributed as follows: Beatrice stockholders received $50 a share, a handsome 45 percent premium over the market price at which the stock traded just one month before the deal was closed. The "marriage brokers" (KKR, Drexel, Kidder Peabody, Lazard Freres, and Salomon Brothers) received $162 million in fees. Mr. Kelly, the new Beatrice CEO, was paid $6.75 million for his work in planning the buyout, an additional $13 million "for advising himself" on the strategy of breaking Beatrice into 10 salable parts, and a $1.3 million annual salary. Finally, $22 million in golden parachutes was paid to Beatrice's top six executives to obtain their consent to taking the company private.

Two factors would determine the success of the venture: first, management's ability to generate sufficient cash flow to cover the crushing interest burden; and second, management's ability to sell off major chunks of the company at attractive prices in order to reduce the sizable debt as quickly as possible. Then, if all went well, what remained of Beatrice could be "taken public" again; that is, it could be sold to a new set of stockholders—hopefully at a handsome profit.

By the end of 1988, part of the objective had been met. Nine subsidiaries of the old Beatrice had been sold, demonstrating that the separate parts of a humpty-dumpty conglomerate are worth more than the whole (see Table 7). Still to be sold were assets of the U.S. Food subsidiary valued at approximately $3 billion: Hunt-Wesson, Swift-Eckrich, La Choy, and Butterball.

The utter incongruity of it all was perhaps best captured by Jim

TABLE 7

THE BREAKUP: WHERE THE PIECES WENT

Beatrice Subsidiary	Sale Price ($ millions)	Buyer
1986		
Playtex International (incl. Max Factor and Almay cosmetics)	$1,250	Playtex management
Soft Drink Bottling (regional Coca-Cola bottlers)	1,000	Coca-Cola
Americold (cold storage warehouses)	480	Americold management
Meadow Gold (incl. Louis Sherry and Mountain High)	315	Borden
Avis (car rentals)	263	Wesray Capital
1987		
International Foods (incl. Chipy, Campofrio, Blue Boy)	985	TLC Group
E-II Holdings (consumer products, incl. Samsonite, Culligan, Stiffel)	800*	Management, public
Bottled Water (incl. Great Bear, Arrowhead, Ozarka)	450	Perrier
1988		
Tropicana	1,200	Seagram

* Plus approximately $700 million in stock distributed to Beatrice shareholders.
Source: *Business Week*, May 9, 1988, p. 99.

Hightower, Texas commissioner of agriculture, who observed that a small group of people, "who couldn't make a biscuit if someone kneaded the dough," were now in control of one of the nation's largest food conglomerates.[3] Referring to Beatrice's Rosarita line of Mexican foods, another industry observer said: "The guys at the top don't care about selling taco sauce. They are playing a high-stakes game of Monopoly. They are trying to make a million by selling Park Place."[4]

But the blockbuster deal of them all came in October 1988, when F. Ross Johnson, chief executive officer of RJR-Nabisco, the nation's 19th largest industrial concern, unveiled a $17 billion bid to buy the firm from its stockholders and to take it private. Johnson had risen to the top of Standard Brands and then sold it to Nabisco. He then rose to the top of Nabisco, and sold it to R. J. Reynolds. Now, Johnson sought control of the RJR-Nabisco empire in order to break the firm apart and to capitalize on the value he had created (using his stockholders' funds). Johnson and a small group of top executives personally stood to profit enormously if the deal went through: *Each* of them would receive fees, equity options, and bonuses potentially worth more than $100 million.

Four days after Johnson launched his deal, however, Kohlberg Kravis Roberts entered the fray. Vowing to protect its "franchise" as the nation's premier buyout operator, KKR unleashed a $21 billion counteroffer for RJR-Nabisco—$4 billion more than what Johnson had offered. For six weeks Johnson and Kohlberg Kravis fought a withering battle, including a disinformation campaign and a diversionary ski trip to Colorado by Henry Kravis designed to lull the Johnson camp into complacency. Along the way another buyout firm, Forstmann Little, entered the battle with the backing of three corporate sponsors (including Ralston Purina and Proctor & Gamble). Feverish bidding and counterbidding drove the offers higher, constantly setting—and breaking—new records.

Acting as arbiter between the bids, RJR-Nabisco's board of directors became increasingly turned off by the magnitude of the personal gains that Johnson had so confidently arranged for himself and for his management partners. The board's resolve not to cave in to management stiffened. The denouement came in the wee hours of November 30: Johnson lost, and the board chose Kohlberg Kravis Roberts as the winner, with its record-breaking offer of $25.1 billion.

The value of this single deal exceeded the combined value of *all* LBOs in the United States for the two years 1984 and 1985. It was so huge that the electronic transfer of funds necessary to complete the deal exceeded the physical capacity of the Federal Reserve Bank's wire transfer system! Yet the billions of dollars thrown around during Johnson's tenure at Nabisco and RJR did not find their way into investment in modernization and new plant and equipment: By the early 1980s, Nabisco's bakery technology had fallen far behind that of some of its smallest rivals, and even today the firm continues to use machinery of superannuated vintage.

For one banker, the RJR deal seemed a story of "capitalism gone mad." Other comments were equally unflattering. "This has gone too far. Too many people making too much money with too much debt," said Wall Street consultant Peter L. Bernstein.[5] The steep runup of buyout prices, said a North Carolina banker, "has all the earmarks of financial gymnastics, and somebody is going to lose their grip on the bar."[6] "Seldom have greed and ego, common features of Wall Street life, been so nakedly on display," observed *Business Week*'s Chris Welles. It's an "unseemly spectacle of deal aspirants fighting like kids in a sandbox for the right to reap millions in profits, not by creating anything but by tearing apart one of the nation's best-known companies."[7] "A healthy appetite for profits is what makes capitalism work," commented Stephen Koepp, *Time*'s business editor. "But at these levels, is it just a power game, in which money is a means of keeping score and the deals themselves are sometimes pointless and destructive?"[8]

In his classic *Wealth of Nations*, Adam Smith pointed to an organizational defect in joint stock companies (the corporations of his day). The directors of such companies, he wrote, "being the managers rather of other people's money than of their own, it cannot well be expected that they should watch over it with the same anxious vigilance with which the partners in a private copartnery frequently watch over their own. Like the stewards of a rich man, they are apt to consider attention to small matters as not for their master's honour, and very easily give themselves a dispensation from having it. Negligence and profusion, therefore, must always prevail, more or less, in the management of the affairs of such a company."[9]

A century and a half later, Adolf A. Berle and Gardiner C. Means diagnosed a similar defect in the modern corporation. The modern corporation, they argued, comprises two "opposing groups, ownership on the one side, control on the other—a control which tends to move further and further away from ownership and ultimately to lie in the hands of the management itself, a management capable of perpetuating its own position. The concentration of economic power separate from ownership has, in fact, created economic empires, and has delivered these empires into the hands of a new form of absolutism, relegating, 'owners' to the position of those who supply the means whereby the new princes may exercise their power."[10]

In the modern corporation, therefore, the stockholder is left "with little more than the loose expectation that a group of men, under a nominal duty to run the enterprise for his benefit and that of others like him, will actually observe this obligation. In almost no particular is [the stockholder] in a position to demand that [managers] do or refrain from doing any given thing. Only in extreme cases will their judgment as to what is or is not to [the stockholder's] interest be interfered with. And they have acquired under the corporate charter power to do many things which by no possibility can be considered in his interest—whether or not they can be considered in the interest of the enterprise as a whole."[11]

Not to despair, however. The separation of ownership from management is not an unbridgeable gulf. Thanks to a novel device in corporate capitalization, discovered by Wall Street wizards and apotheosized by the "new learning" savants, we can return to the

Golden Age when ownership and management were united. That miraculous device is the management-led leveraged buyout (LBO). In essence, it is a "raid from the inside," engineered by management against its own company to wrest control from the company's stockholders.

According to its protagonists, LBOs are an ideal instrument for achieving "asset redeployment," "corporate restructuring," and "deconglomeration." These virtues are said to flow from the fact that the owner-managers of the enterprise now have a greater stake in the business and an enhanced incentive to cut costs, take risks, promote innovation, and eliminate redundant operations. The owner-managers, it is said, "are likely to reallocate company resources with a sharper eye on return on investment, often selling assets or closing operations that don't pay their way or don't fit with the company's basic strategy, and disposing of high-priced assets that fetch more through a sale than through continued use. . . . Managers often do better and work harder because they 'are freed from a more bureaucratic environment and the need to focus constantly on near-term earnings.' "[12] Finally, because of the heavy debt burden they incurred in buying the company, says Professor Michael Jensen, they will be "walking on a razor's edge, and that means they have to work harder."[13]

Whatever the verisimilitude of these claims, leveraged buyouts raise some nettlesome issues:

Do stockholders get a fair price? Metromedia is a telling case in point. The company was taken private by its president John Kluge and a group of associates in June 1984 and promptly dismantled. The results? In two years, according to analyst Benjamin Stein, "Kluge and companions have realized about $4.65 billion from the Metromedia assets they have sold so far, and as noted they still retain various properties. In other words, they paid the stockholders $724 million for a company in May 1984 that by June 1986 turned out to be worth at least six times that amount, with more assets yet to be sold. . . . Or, looked at on a per-share basis, the company for which Kluge paid $38 in cash and notes turned out to be worth, in an orderly liquidation, at least $200 in cash or very short-term notes. . . . Kluge paid no more than $1.3 billion for assets that proved in short order to be worth at least three times that amount. . . . Or, to put it in bottom-line terms, John W. Kluge made a profit of about $3 billion on an investment in which he had to put down no cash at all. The profit was made entirely by paying the stockholders of the formerly public Metromedia about one-sixth of what their company was worth."[14] Commented *Fortune*: "Everybody admits belatedly that Kluge is some sort of business genius. . . . But how much is genius worth? $3 *billion*? And how much of this prescience did he impart to his stockholders?"[15]

Are the architects of a management-led buyout likely to be "fair"? Not usually. The problem "is simply this," says former SEC Commissioner Bevis Longstreth: "Management is acting on both sides of the transaction. In its fiduciary capacity, management is seeking to sell the corporation and, therefore, must have concluded that a sale is in the best interests of the shareholders. In its proprietary capacity, management is seeking to purchase the corporation, and must have concluded that it can do so at a price favorable to it. In short management is dealing with itself."[16] How, one may ask, can management serve two masters and be equally loyal to each?

What about the "fairness" issue when a company is taken private, its assets stripped, and then it is resold to the public in a reverse LBO? In a now legendary case, the Gibson Greeting Card Company "was taken private in 1982, then a year-and-a-half later taken public again. A management group led by Wesray Capital Corp. bought Gibson from RCA Corp. in 1982 for $80 million, putting up only $1 million of its own capital. Reportedly, without major changes in the company—although perhaps benefitting by the bull market which began in 1982—the going public price, just a year-and-a-half later, was $290 million. One of the Wesray principals, former Treasury Secretary William Simon, saw his personal investment rise from $330,000 to $66 million in cash and stock."[17] In cases of this sort, says Daniel S. O'Connell, co-head of leveraged buyouts at First Boston, "managements see that pot of gold" and tell their investment bankers, "Let's do it."[18]

What about bondholders? *Business Week* says that the LBO craze, "is slaughtering owners of high-grade corporate bonds."[19] Some finance officers consider it a simple "bondholder rip-off." "Screwing the bondholder is the very stuff that LBO's are made of," comments *Fortune*.[20] The reason? In consummating an LBO, there is a large-scale exchange of debt for equity (leveraging) and the substitution of lower-quality debt for higher-quality debt. As the new higher-risk debt (junk bonds) is laid on top of the old debt (high-grade bonds), the value of the old debt declines: "Between 1984 and 1988 there were 254 downgrades of industrial debt by Moody's Investors Service as a result of takeovers, buyouts, or defensive maneuvers by companies borrowing heavily to avoid a raid. The rating agency estimates that $160 billion worth of bonds have been downgraded, clipping bondholders for at least $13 billion. Not surprisingly, these creditors are talking about 'theft.' "[21]

What about the effects of leveraging on the balance sheet of the new company sired by the LBO? What are the consequences of the extraordinary insouciance with which debt is substituted for equity? Leveraging is not for the faint of heart; it is a game of Russian roulette. In the case of the R.H. Macy buyout, for example, the company's balance sheet was drastically transmuted: "Total debt, only $144 million in early May [1986], rose to $3.2 billion. Total debt-to-capital, likewise, jumped from 8.9 percent to 92.0 percent. Net interest expense was forecast to average $625 million through 1990 versus an average of $76 million in the 1981–85 period, and the company forecast no profit until 1990."[22] Clearly, the staggering interest burden imposed on the "newco" has to be covered by a steady cash flow. LBO proponents view this as positive because it disciplines the new company, forcing it to cut costs, trim overhead, and eliminate fat. But what if, in order to meet interest payments, the firm has to cut bone as well as fat? What if it is unable to invest in vital R&D or new plant and equipment to stay competitive? What if a recession precipitates a decline in profits, or interest rates go up, or both occur simultaneously?

Does a leveraged buyout protect management from the constant pressure of shareholders and the investment community to increase the market value of the corporation's stock? Does the LBO therefore liberate management to concentrate on decisions that will produce long-run benefits to the company? Or does the highly leveraged buyout, and the defensive responses to it, force companies to focus on the short-term bottom line rather than on capital investment or long-term planning, research, and development? The matter is the subject of lively dispute among corporate executives. One skeptic is Gino Pala, president and chief executive officer of Dixon Ticonderoga. "If you thought you were under pressure from stockholders," he counsels managers of LBO companies, "you haven't seen anything yet." After the LBO, you are "going to be dealing with bankers . . . [You'll] be in worse shape. Loan covenants, deadlines. With shareholders, you're not under pressure to meet interest payments. Pressure from shareholders doesn't put you out of business. Pressure from these other guys does."[23]

Are LBOs nothing more than a tax play? The arithmetic, some say, is straightforward and simple: interest on indebtedness is tax deductible; the higher the interest burden, the more of a corporation's revenue is sheltered from the corporate income tax. Therefore, from the corporation's point of view, it is cheaper to finance investments with debt rather than equity. The higher the leverage (ratio of debt to equity), the smaller the tax liability. In the event, many LBO companies are so highly leveraged that they have no tax obligation at all for several years after the buyout; indeed, under the carryback provisions of the tax code, they may be eligible for a refund on the income taxes they paid in the years preceding the buyout. (That certainly was the case in the buyout of RJR-Nabisco.) It raises the question if, and to what extent, leveraged buyouts enjoy a hidden tax subsidy. *Forbes* has no doubt about the answer: "Uncle Sam is providing a $5 billion subsidy for the needy folks who want to take over RJR-Nabisco. . . . A billion or so will go into the pockets of Wall Street lawyers, accountants, corporate managers, bond salesmen and other deserving types in the form of fees, markups and profits; the rest will go into the pockets of RJR-Nabisco's former shareholders. Thank you, Mr. Sucker Taxpayer. Through a quirk in the tax code, the federal government subsidizes leveraged takeovers."[24]

Finally, why put together what is shortly thereafter put asunder? This is the "Humpty-Dumpty" problem. It raises the fundamental question whether playing the acquisition-buyout game benefits the U.S. economy. If, for example, it made sense for Beatrice to consummate a series of acquisitions and painstakingly build a gargantuan conglomerate, combining under the same umbrella Playtex brassieres and Americold warehouses, La Choy chow mein and Stiffel lamps, Samsonite luggage and Tropicana orange juice, Max Factor cosmetics and Culligan water softener, does it make sense to engineer a leveraged buyout to restore the status quo ante by breaking the whole into separate and independent constituent parts? Is it rational (or indeed credible) for R. J. Reynolds to claim in September 1985 that the acquisition of Nabisco (Oreo cookies, Planter's peanuts, Baby Ruth candy bars, etc.) was a marriage made in heaven, only to insist in December 1988 that a divorce was in the best interest of the erstwhile marriage partners as well as society at large? Only one or the other course of action makes economic sense. Only one or the other can be conducive to enhanced efficiency, technological progress, and superior competitiveness in world markets.

5

THE ESTABLISHMENTARIANS

We find everywhere a type of organization . . . in which the higher officials are plodding and dull, those less senior are active only in intrigue against each other, and the junior men are frustrated or frivolous. Little is being attempted. Nothing is being achieved.

—*Parkinson's Law*

LTV is a huge conglomerate firm that literally emerged from nowhere in the 1960s. As of the mid-1950s, in fact, LTV's annual corporate sales were so small ($1.5 million) that it failed to make even the list of the 1,000 largest American firms. By 1968, however, LTV ranked as the 22nd largest industrial corporation in the country. Its rise to the pinnacle of American industry was the product of a succession of large mergers and acquisitions, including Wilson & Co. (meatpacking and sporting goods), Chance-Vought Aircraft Co., Okonite, and Braniff Airways.

Steel production is one part of the far-flung conglomerate empire LTV has assembled. In 1968, LTV acquired Jones & Laughlin Steel Company, at the time the nation's 6th largest steel concern, producing 7.7 million tons of steel per year, and with assets in excess of $1 billion. A decade later, in 1978, LTV acquired another major steel firm, Youngstown Sheet & Tube, the nation's 8th largest steel producer at the time. As a result of these acquisitions, LTV was the country's 3rd largest steel manufacturer by the early 1980s. It obviously had become a colossus in the field.

But LTV's steel operations were hemorrhaging badly. Its losses were mounting, while its competitiveness declined. In an effort to staunch the red ink, and in an attempt to boost its economic performance, LTV stunned industry analysts in late 1983 by announcing its decision to acquire Republic Steel—the nation's 5th biggest steel producer, and a firm whose economic troubles matched those of LTV—in a friendly merger valued at $700 million. With this merger, LTV moved up to second place in the American steel industry, just behind U.S. Steel Corporation.

In its annual report for the year, LTV proclaimed that its acquisition of Republic Steel would "significantly improve the efficiency of our steel operations, with resulting long-term benefits for shareholders, customers and employees." The combined resources of the consolidated firms, LTV said, "will create a stronger steel operation than either can accomplish as a stand-alone company. Realignment and rationalization of the merged raw material and steelmaking facilities will greatly reduce costs, improve capacity utilization, increase productivity and enable us to make more efficient use of scarce capital." It would stand, LTV management boasted, as "a landmark in the annals of America's basic industries as they strive to compete in the modern world marketplace."

The top managers of America's corporate complexes sit at the apex of the largest, most influential organizations in the country. To describe the firms they manage as states within a state is no exaggeration. Measured by annual dollar receipts, Exxon is bigger than California by a third, and three times larger than the state of Texas. General Motors is bigger than Michigan, Ohio, and Pennsylvania *combined*. At times the nation's largest industrial corporation, at times the second largest, GM can boast of 876,000 employees, approximately 1 million stockholders, sales of $103 billion, $72 billion in assets, and net profits of $3 billion. As described by one Detroit executive, "General Motors is the kind of institution whose like doesn't exist elsewhere in Western civilization. It is America's Japan." The value added of giants like Exxon, General Motors, and IBM exceeds that of most nations of the world.

The top managements of America's 200 largest industrial firms—a group any moderately sized auditorium could comfortably accommodate—collectively preside over 43 percent of the nation's value added in manufacturing, and 61 percent of its total corporate manufacturing assets.[1] Because they direct multistate, multiplant production operations, their decisions have a profound impact on the welfare of communities and states, and on the health of the economy as a whole. The kinds of products they choose to produce, the investments they choose to make, the plants they choose to build and keep running, the research and development they choose to undertake—all these decisions critically affect the nation's economic performance. They have a profound influence on our ability to generate jobs, on the standard of living, on the rate of technological advance, and on our international competitiveness (or lack thereof).

At the same time, the vast size of these corporate complexes gives them considerable political clout. Procter & Gamble, for example is the nation's 17th largest industrial concern: "The company's sheer size—$15.5 billion in annual sales, almost 75,000 employees, plants in more than 50 cities and towns across the U.S.—gives P&G tremendous access [to government]. . . . Its facilities are spread over 25 states, giving it ready entree to about half the members of the Senate. On the House side, almost 20% of the 435 members have a P&G plant in or near their districts. . . . There's a P&G facility in Forth Worth—home base of [former] House Speaker James Wright, D-Tex.—and another in Modesto, which is represented by [former] House Majority Whip Tony Coelho, D-California. A quarter of the membership of the tax-writing House Ways and Means Committee represents a municipality containing a P&G plant." Describing a legislative dinner sponsored by the firm, one congressman recounts: "They had a map on the wall of where all their installations were. . . . I looked around the room, and you should have seen how many members of Congress were there. There were people from California, people there from New York—and from every place in between."[2]

For the chieftains of big business, faith in the economic virtues of giant corporate size is fundamental. According to the Business Roundtable, an organization composed of chief executive officers of 200 of the very largest American firms, giant firms are "an integral and important part of the total economic picture. The country's economy could not function as it does without big enterprises that are large enough to have the assets, the credit and the talent to be able to think and act long term. Such companies can direct their planning, research and finance in ways which . . . will enable them to become corporations for all seasons—companies capable of responding to and meeting the nation's needs through good times and bad."[3] Corporate bigness, they insist, "enables the business enterprise to have a policy and to have a special policy-making body which is sufficiently removed from the actual day-to-day problems to take the long view, and to take into account the relationship between the organization and society."[4] Bigness, they believe, "has the means, capabilities, and experience to perform large-scale economic tasks in a socially responsible manner when given the opportunity and flexibility to do so."[5]

Top managements of these industrial empires are not averse to corporate mergers, acquisitions, and consolidations—provided *they* are the ones who initiate the deals, and so long as the deals are conducted in "friendly" fashion. In fact, during the 1960s and 1970s, the nation's 200 largest industrial firms typically accounted for 50 to 60 percent of the very largest corporate mergers consummated (acquisitions valued at $10 million or more), a pattern that concentrated even greater control over the country's manufacturing base in the hands of fewer, bigger firms. According to the Business Roundtable, this is as it should be, because the leaders of big business "are seasoned veterans of one or many mergers and acquisitions." They "know from hands-on experience that mergers and acquisitions can be a useful and productive mechanism which is helpful in maximizing efficiency in the marketplace." Friendly mergers are "useful mechanisms by which corporations can expand and grow and their efficiency and profitability can be improved." Such friendly fusions, they insist, "are conducted with careful thought, concern for the corporate constituents, the free exchange of information to assure informal negotiation, and negotiations that provide the surest means of arriving at a price that is fair to all."[6]

The LTV-Republic consolidation is precisely the friendly kind of merger the Business Roundtable applauds. But incumbent managements have nothing but contempt for raiders who launch hostile takeover assaults on their firms. They denounce the raiders on at least six grounds:

First, as they see them, hostile raids are dangerously speculative games of financial chicanery. "Once before in this century we lost sight of what business and corporations were all about," the Business Roundtable warns. "That was in the 1920s when—as now—the game was playing with corporations rather than running them, and it was dominated, not by entrepreneurs and managers, but by people interested only in fast returns on speculative risks. We all know the consequences of that exercise in corporate game playing. What reason is there to think the end result of this round of the game will be any different?"[7]

Second, this speculative profiteering is facilitated by junk bonds—what incumbent managements call "a destructive new weapon in the corporate raiders' arsenal." Junk bonds, they say, enable corporate raiders to borrow virtually 100 percent of the cost of an acquisition in advance, with little or no security, on the promise that they will break up the target company to repay the loan. According to Fred L. Hartley, president of Unocal, and the target of a hostile takeover raid, junk bonds "are weapons created and used solely for the corporate quick kill. With them, a raider can convert a company's equity into debt, slash research . . . milk assets and take the money and run."[8]

Third, incumbent managements argue that the raiders' fast-buck, quick-kill profiteering destroys good economic performance. The chairman of the Phillips Petroleum Company, a target of two successive hostile raids, compares the raiders to "a farmer who does not rotate his crops, does not periodically let his land lie fallow, does not fertilize his land by planting cover and creating wind breaks. In the early years, he will maximize his return from the land. . . . But inevitably it leads to a dust bowl and economic disaster. . . . Day after day, the takeover entrepreneurs are maximizing their returns at the expense of future generations that will not benefit from the research and development and capital investments that takeover entrepreneurs are forcing businesses to forego."[9] The chairman of Goodyear Tire & Rubber warns that under the Damocles sword of hostile takeovers, "Long-term planning and long-term investment will become relics of the past, and so will any hope of a significant American position in the arena of global competition."[10] As he sees it, "America's economic strength was built on the bedrock of long-term commitments, not on the crumbled clay of one-night stands."[11]

Fourth, regarding the raiders' claim that they train their gunsights on underperforming managements, David M. Roderick, chairman of U.S. Steel Corporation, expresses grave doubts "whether the financial paper pushers have a demonstrated track record that would qualify them to identify inefficient management." He asks, "Have they manifested their managerial skills so that we can with confidence entrust these financiers with more efficiently and effectively running a target enterprise?"[12]

Fifth, incumbent managements warn that hostile raids are burying American firms under mountains of debt, which further erodes economic performance and renders the economy more susceptible to a financial collapse. Even when target firms are able to fend off the raiders, incumbent managements argue, the surviving firm is mortally wounded; it will be financially devastated, highly leveraged with debt, and vulnerable to economic downturns, while important decisions concerning R&D and capital investment will have been delayed and distorted because of the distractions of fighting off unwanted suitors.

Sixth, incumbent managements contend that the important constituencies of large corporations comprise far more than the stockholders alone, and that the interests of these other groups—employees, customers, suppliers, communities—are ignored by takeover "buccaneers." According to Goodyear Tire & Rubber, "All of these constituencies must be served fairly. . . . All, in one way or another, are stakeholders in the company. Their destinies are interwoven in many ways, including the broad issue of American industry's ability to be internationally competitive."[13]

In sum, as incumbent management sees them, the corporate raiders are nothing but financial barbarians—modern-day pirates. The "raiders are wreaking havoc with U.S. industry, reducing competition and throwing thousands of skilled people out of work. . . . Raiders have looted target companies, taken immense personal profits, and left remaining stockholders crushed with new debt. . . . These raids and bust-up takeovers have not inspired one new technological innovation; they have just drained off investment capital. They have not strengthened companies; they have weakened them . . . they have not strengthened the nation's economy; they have weakened it."[14] The raiders are plunderers. They can tear down, but they cannot build up. They are enemies of the nation's economic vitality, and a deadly threat to its future.

But what of big managements' own economic performance? Viewed in the light of their track record over the past two decades, criticisms of the raiders by incumbent managements seem more than a little hypocritical, and rather blatantly self-serving.

For example, haven't incumbent managements built up big, bloated bureaucracies poorly suited for effective economic performance? Haven't they spawned what Richard Darman, former investment banker and now director of the Bush administration's Office of Management and the Budget, has criticized as "corporacy"—that is, "corporate America's tendency to be like the government bureaucracy that corporate executives love to malign: bloated, risk-averse, inefficient and unimaginative."[15] In their candid moments, some chief executives admit as much. Former GM president

Elliott M. Estes once confided: "Chevrolet is such a big monster that you twist its tail and nothing happens at the other end for months and months. It is so gigantic that there isn't any way to really run it. You just sort of try to keep track of it."[16] Even current GM chief executive Roger Smith confesses that the main reason for the failures of the American automobile industry "was not exchange rates, differential tax burdens or other external economic factors. . . . It was management—of both people and work processes."[17]

Hasn't the poor performance of these lumbering bureaucracies inflicted substantial damage on the economy? In automobiles and steel, for example, the inefficiencies, high costs, low productivity, and technological stagnation of corporate bigness have led to the loss of markets at home and abroad, massive plant closings, layoffs of hundreds of thousands of workers, and economic devastation for scores of afflicted communities across the country. More generally, the Fortune 500 firms collectively *lost* an estimated 4 to 5 million jobs between 1970 and 1985—this at a time when the rest of the economy created 30 million new jobs. Is this what the chieftains of big business mean when they wax eloquent about their deep concern for their broader constituencies and "stakeholders"? Is this congruent with their self-proclaimed superiority at engaging in long-term planning? Does their own record support the claim that they are best qualified to direct America's economic affairs?

What about the deplorable record of failed "friendly" mergers, acquisitions, and consolidations effectuated by these same chieftains of big business? Examining the merger record of 33 large, prestigious U.S. firms over the period 1950 to 1986, Michael Porter describes their performance as "dismal."[18] More than half the acquisitions they made subsequently failed and were sold off. For conglomerate acquisitions, the record was even worse—a startling 74 percent failure rate. The failure rates of the mergers they consummated include: ITT (52%), General Foods (63%), General Electric (65%), Xerox (71%), General Mills (75%), RCA (80%), and CBS (87%).

Haven't these "friendly" mergers and acquisitions wasted stockholders' funds, exacerbated the burden of corporate bureaucracy, and aggravated poor economic performance? Evaluating Goodyear Tire & Rubber's conglomerate acquisition spree, for example, British raider Sir James Goldsmith points out that top management "strayed into industries about which it knew nothing, jeopardizing the very heart of Goodyear's business and the security of all those associated with it." With compelling logic, he claims that the approximately $2 billion Goodyear spent on conglomerate acquisitions "should have been invested to build the most modern, state-of-the-art, frontier-breaking industrial infrastructure to produce better tires, cheaper, and to ensure that Goodyear's operations could compete with anything, including imports, no matter what their origin. Instead the market share for imported tires rose from 12 percent in 1982 to 24 percent in 1985 in the replacement tire market."[19]

And what of LTV-Republic? Two years after the deal, in 1986, the LTV-Republic combine collapsed in the single biggest corporate bankruptcy in American business history! In clinical fashion, the *Wall Street Journal* observed that the firm's disastrous postmerger performance calls "into question the premise behind some large mergers—that the combined resources of two ailing companies can create more strength than either could muster alone."[20] It demonstrated that when you combine two losers, you create an even bigger loser.

Finally, haven't incumbent managements presided over corporations as if they were their personal fiefdoms, replete with golf courses, sumptuous corporate headquarters, and a personal air force of private jets? Haven't they built monuments to gratify their egos, rather than forging world-class competitive economic organizations? In a front-page cover story examining LTV's woes, for example, the *Wall Street Journal* reports: "LTV Corp. is fighting to survive, but you'd never know that from its posh new corporate headquarters here [in Dallas] atop the 50-story LTV Center. A gleaming black marble staircase swirls through three of LTV's five floors, and original Western paintings grace mahogany walls. LTV Chairman Raymond Hay calls it 'one of the most prestigious landmarks west of the Mississippi River.' "[21] Haven't incumbent managements exploited their "stakeholders" in providing for their own palatial lifestyles—luxuriating in lavish, million-dollar compensation rates virtually divorced from performance, and three times greater than the amounts paid their Japanese counterparts?[22] Have they not, as a result, become insulated, isolated, and out of touch with the realities of the marketplace, and the preferences of the customers it is ostensibly their duty to serve? And are not incumbent managements responsible for allowing all this to occur on their watch?

6

THE MARRIAGE BROKERS

Investment banking has become to productive enterprise in this country what mud wrestling is to the performing arts.
—Mark Russell

They are the marriage brokers—the advisers, facilitators, implementers and, in the view of some analysts, the prime instigators of corporate mergers and takeovers. They counsel and advise those who have decided to do a deal. They also develop and peddle deals of their own creation. They are the Wall Street investment houses that play the M&A game.

Financiers played a key role in consolidating American industry during the great turn-of-the-century corporate merger wave. J. P. Morgan himself personally effected scores of mergers, creating such dominant firms as General Electric, AT&T, International Harvester, and the "combination of combinations"—the United States Steel Corporation, the nation's first billion-dollar industrial firm. But branded as "malefactors of great wealth," robber barons, and the Money Trust, the great financiers were later shattered by the speculative financial excesses of the 1920s and the economic catastrophes that followed in the 1930s. They were exposed, embarrassed, and to a considerable degree discredited in a succession of government investigations.[1] (In his first inaugural address in 1933, Franklin Delano Roosevelt castigated "the unscrupulous money changers" who "have no vision," who "know only the rules of a generation of self-seekers," who "have fled from their high seats in the temple of our civilization," and who "stand indicted in the court of public opinion.")

Subjected to government regulation and oversight, for the next four decades the great investment banks confined themselves to what would become their traditional role of underwriting new stock and bond issues, bringing those issues to market in an orderly fashion, providing ancillary financial advice, and writing prospectuses. Typically specialized by function and field, and habitually allied with customary clients, the investment banks served as intermediaries between users and suppliers of financial capital.

During the 1960s, the "go-go" conglomerate merger craze attracted some investment bankers back into the field of corporate fusions. Prominent among these was Felix Rohatyn of Lazard Freres, who guided ITT's conglomerate campaign in acquiring Avis, the Hartford Insurance Company, Bobbs-Merrill Publishers, Sheraton Hotels, Levitt & Co. builders, and Continental Baking (of Wonder bread fame). Others, such as Morgan Stanley, the descendant of the original House of Morgan, moved cautiously into the merger and acquisition field during the 1970s. It was First Boston, however, one of the oldest of the investment banks, that dramatically demonstrated the vast, virtually costless vein of gold that could be mined in corporate M&A. Leading the firm was what became its brilliant "dynamic duo" of deal-makers, Joseph Perella and Bruce Wasserstein.

Perella joined First Boston in 1972 as an older, but freshly minted Harvard MBA. The following year he took a newly created position as the firm's merger and acquisition specialist, after being told that he was too old for a "regular career path." Wasserstein's background is more colorful (and more contradictory): A veritable child prodigy, Wasserstein had by age 24 earned MBA and law degrees from Harvard and a postgraduate degree in economics from Cambridge University. Fresh out of Harvard Law School, Wasserstein initially had joined Ralph Nader's "raiders" to co-author a scathing indictment of the country's moribund antitrust effort, including—ironically—its failures in combatting corporate mergers and acquisitions! (The resulting book, *The Closed Enterprise System*, was published in 1972. It concludes: "Until the existing anti-antitrust consensus is reversed, we grope about in economic darkness . . . [and] mock our lofty commitments to free enterprise and equal justice. If business and Washington shun the question, aroused citizens and lawyers and economists must raise it: 'Whatever happened to antitrust?' ") In 1977, Wasserstein was recruited by Perella to work for First Boston; he switched from battling corporate mergers to implementing and facilitating them.

Led by Perella and Wasserstein, First Boston's participation in the late 1970s in just two corporate mergers netted the firm $3 million in fees in a single month. Its appetite whetted by these lucrative gains, First Boston quickly expanded its M&A operation. It hit pay dirt in a big way in 1981: For advising Du Pont in its acquisition of Conoco, and for representing Marathon Oil in its "white knight" acquisition by U.S. Steel in order to escape the clutches of Mobil Oil, First Boston garnered fees of $32 million on these two deals alone—fees that accounted for the bulk of the investment bank's record earnings of $46.3 million in 1981.[2] First Boston was on a roll. As Perella pointed out at the time, its fees from mergers and acquisitions in 1981 "were triple those in 1980, which in turn were double those in 1979."[3]

Chagrined that First Boston was not devoting enough attention and prestige to its M&A operation, in 1988 Wasserstein and Perella shocked the firm by quitting and forming their own financial operation, Wasserstein-Perella. From the start, the new firm attracted star clients; it served as financial intermediary in Philip Morris's acquisition of Kraft, and in Campeau's acquisition of Federated Department Stores in 1988.

Another investment bank, Drexel Burnham Lambert, also struck gold in corporate deal-making, but it did so in an unconventional way—a way that old-line investment banks initially considered as outside the bounds of genteel responsibility. Led by its young *wunderkind*, Michael Milken, Drexel Burnham in the 1970s pioneered the junk bond market that, in the 1980s, would become the lifeblood of corporate raiders and leveraged-buyout artists. As an MBA student at the Wharton School, Milken became convinced that junk bonds—high-risk, low-grade debt issued by small firms and newcomers, and shunned by the elite banking houses—offered returns far outweighing their risks. After joining Drexel in the early 1970s, Milken put his theory into practice. He developed junk bonds into a vast national market where fledgling firms lacking track records could raise funds for investment and expansion. The market Milken assembled (which he preferred to call "high-yield" rather than "junk") was immensely profitable: Its success propelled Drexel Burnham from the minor leagues to become the nation's 7th largest investment bank by 1983.

It was in 1983 that Milken took a fateful step—one that revolutionized the economic landscape, and shook it to its foundations. Having moved his junk bond operation from New York to Beverly Hills, Milken redirected it to the financing of assaults on some of the nation's biggest and best-known corporations (including raids on Gulf Oil, Phillips Petroleum, Revlon, Walt Disney, and Union Carbide). No longer would Drexel peddle junk bonds issued by others; now it would "manufacture" and market junk bonds of its own making. Milken unleashed a financial juggernaut—a money machine able on a few days notice to line up billions of dollars to fund corporate raids, takovers, and leveraged buyouts.

By 1984, Drexel Burnham was the nation's second largest financial underwriter of corporate stocks and bonds. Shocked by Drexel's ungentlemanly aggressive tactics and its involvement in hostile raids, the banking fraternity branded the firm "the Libya of investment banking," while its annual conference for its junk bond clients was dubbed the Predator's Ball. But one fact was indisputable: Drexel Burnham's revenues and profits were exploding exponentially, and partners in the firm were carting home millions of dollars in annual bonuses.[4] In 1987, Milken's income reached $550 million—equivalent to $1.5 million per day.

Lured by these spectacular gains, the other major investment banks—Salomon Bros., Merrill Lynch, Goldman Sachs, Lehman Bros., Kidder Peabody—geared up to play the enormously profitable new merger game. In the early 1980s, M&A shops were transformed from small back-room operations run as sideline services for regular clients into major units rivaling in size the banks' traditional divisions. A generation of staid, pinstripe-suited investment bankers was replaced by smart, young, hyperaggressive deal-makers. Gone too was the notion of long-term client associations and loyalty. As one top deal-maker put it in 1986, "We don't serve anyone anymore."[5]

The ten largest of these M&A factories are shown in Table 8, indicating the number and value of corporate deals they handled in 1987 and 1988. They are an oligopoly of deal-makers. The three largest—First Boston, Morgan Stanley, and Goldman Sachs—together handle fully one-third of the mergers and acquisitions valued at $100 million or more. The seven largest collectively account for some 60 percent of the entire business.

These investment banks provide an almost limitless variety of merger and acquisition services: For corporations looking to buy other firms, they advise on how to hold the acquisition price down; for corporations looking to be acquired, they advise on how to push the acquisition price up. They devise tactics designed to stampede a sale (such as two-tiered tender offers that pay more to those who sell out early). At the other extreme, they design tactics to deter mergers and takeovers (such as poison pills, scorched earth strategies, and lockup options). They provide analyses, profiles of partners (actual or potential), and "what-if" scenarios. They have teams of specialists with expertise concentrated by geographic region, by industry, and by particular types of deals (such as acquisitions or divestitures). They can draw from their in-house stock and bond

TABLE 8

LEADING ADVISERS FOR MERGERS AND ACQUISITIONS, 1987–1988

	Number of Deals		Value of Deals ($ billions)	
	1987	1988	1987	1988
Goldman Sachs	134	158	$ 63.5	$ 93.4
First Boston	174	153	55.1	78.2
Shearson Lehman	164	211	25.6	74.1
Morgan Stanley	120	125	42.3	74.1
Merrill Lynch	101	116	34.3	24.8
Drexel Burnham Lambert	126	158	22.7	39.0
Lazard Freres	44	59	24.3	34.7
Salomon Brothers	76	124	21.9	31.8
Kidder Peabody	70	73	13.5	17.7
Total	1,009	1,177	$303.2	$467.8

Source: *Wall Street Journal,* February 3, 1988, p. 1; *New York Times,* March 7, 1989, p. 33.

trading experience, as well as from their arbitrage operations, to gauge the capital markets' likely reaction to a deal. They can provide advice without committing any capital of their own. Or they can provide bridge financing of hundreds of millions of dollars to facilitate a deal. They can underwrite securities and bonds, and feed them into vast distribution networks. And they can provide "fairness" letters that, depending on the circumstances and the client, will recommend that stockholders accept or reject a proffered deal.

Their services are available to all payers. ("Investment bankers are like a good bird dog," says T. Boone Pickens. "They will hunt with anybody who has a gun."[6]) They may be on a firm's side of the table today, and on the opposite side tomorrow. They profess no national allegiance and are perfectly comfortable advising foreign companies seeking to acquire U.S. firms. And now they are expanding into overseas operations.

Mercenaries for all seasons, they may be called in at the outset to launch a deal; they may join a deal already underway; or they may search for an alternative to a deal already in process. They candidly admit that their object is to be involved in every major deal, whether invited or not.[7] For example, when in 1985 American Hospital Supply disclosed a $2.5 billion merger with Hospital Corporation of America, First Boston "saw a chance to torpedo that deal and replace it with another, larger one." First Boston found another suitor, Baxter Travenol Laboratories, and "put a fifteen-man task force on the case, some of the members working one hundred hours a week, and one of them stationed for the duration in Baxter Travenol's offices. . . . Eventually the AHS board concluded that it had no alternative but to accept the Baxter Travenol bid. . . . Thus a friendly merger among equals was aborted, and replaced by an unwanted but unavoidable takeover orchestrated . . . by the First Boston M&A team."[8] Likewise, "Morgan Stanley's M&A men made no bones about going after merger business, even from nonclients; a group was established to spend its time studying every announced merger and trying to figure out how Morgan Stanley, by finding a better deal or a white knight, could muscle in on the deal, even by approaching a corporation with which it had no previous relationship."[9]

In fact, some of the biggest investment banks have now established "creative directors," assigned the full-time task of devising deals to be marketed to potential takers. First Boston's creative director "reads research reports and dreams up mergers. Then he tries to convince the participants. . . . Like the guy who asks every pretty girl in the hall to dance, [he] gets turned down a lot. . . . But from time to time the girl says yes."[10] Samuel Hayes, professor of investment banking, observes that these deal-makers "are under great pressure to keep finding new revenue sources to feed the monster that's been created. . . . There's been steady movement away from the traditional role as counselor toward activity initiated by the investment banker himself."[11]

The fees of these brokers are geared to each particular deal. When they represent buyers, their fees are structured to provide bonuses if the deal goes through. When they represent sellers, their fees are geared to the acquisition price paid, with huge bonuses if the actual price exceeds the anticipated price. They collect fees for providing advice during a merger. They collect more fees for lining up financing for the deal. They collect fees for underwriting the issue of stocks and bonds in the deal. And they are paid commitment fees and interest for providing bridge financing for the deal.[12]

Moreover, they typically make sure they will be paid and held harmless if a deal subsequently sours. Thus, Goldman Sachs represented Getty Oil, and was at the center of the Texaco–Pennzoil–Getty Oil imbroglio, but Goldman Sachs was subsequently protected by an indemnity clause holding it free from liability—while Texaco was hit with a multibillion-dollar lawsuit for interfering with Pennzoil's intitial agreement to acquire Getty Oil.[13]

Ever-escalating, astronomical fees provide the incentive for investment banks to play the M&A game. "Why are people willing to pay $21 billion for a cracker-and-tobacco company?" asks *Forbes*. "Wrong question. Better ask: Who on Wall Street profits from the madness?"[14]

Whenever the phone rings in a Wall Street M&A shop, it's jingle bells announcing Santa Claus. In the 1980s, M&A divisions have become prime profit centers for investment banks. At Morgan Stanley, for example, the M&A unit (with only 120 of the firm's 5,000 employees) generated 70 percent of its investment banking revenues in 1985, and one-third of its total operating revenues from all sources.[15] At First Boston, analysts estimate that M&A operations account for as much as half of the bank's overall profits.[16]

Of the profitability of this line of work, the head of one M&A operation observes: "Most of the big franchises on the Street do at least $75 million a year in fees . . . and some select firms do in excess of $100 million. Subtract $3 million to $5 million in salaries and overhead from that, and you've got plenty of room for bonuses. Every marginal dollar drops right down to the bottom line."[17] As *Business Week* explains it: "An investment banking team can bring in $10 million or $15 million at a pop for a couple of weeks spent advising on a major deal."[18] Others estimate that a number of investment banks would have suffered financial losses in recent years were it not for the fees generated by their M&A divisions.[19] Table 9 depicts the fees generated for investment banks involved in some selected corporate merger and acquisition deals. Although the precise figures are closely guarded, knowledgeable analysts estimate that the leading banks are now generating M&A fees on the order of $200 to $300 million annually.[20] These sums, as Sherlock Holmes would say, have "a distinctive materiality about them."

The more contested, drawn-out, and convoluted the corporate feeding frenzy becomes, the greater the investment bank fees it throws off. In the Bendix-Martin Marietta-Allied-United Technologies fiasco of 1982, where at one point Bendix and Martin Marietta seemed to have achieved the impossible, with each simultaneously seeming to have taken over the other, the investment bank participants profited handsomely: First Boston garnered $6 to $8 million in fees; Lehman Bros., $5 to $6 million; Salomon Bros., $3 million; Kidder Peabody, $750,000; and Lazard Freres, $700,000.[21]

The Revlon–Pantry Pride brawl, protracted over a three-month period in 1985, at the time was billed by one investment banker as "the deal of the century." It generated fees of $60 million for Drexel Burnham; up to $30 million for Morgan Stanley; $11 million for Lazard Freres; and $3 million for Goldman Sachs.[22] This record was soon eclipsed in the 1987 battle between Campeau and Macy to take over Federated Department Stores. In this single deal—dubbed by one observer the "Wall Street Fair Employment Act"—the total fees generated are estimated to have been as high as $200 million, including $19 million for the First Boston; $20 million for Shearson Lehman; $18 million for Goldman Sachs; $16 million for Hellman & Friedman; and $10 million for Wasserstein-Perella & Co. (the First Boston M&A wizards who in early 1988 set out on their own).[23]

The Federated record was soon shattered in the battle to take over R. J. Reynolds. This single deal may eventually throw off total investment bank fees as high as $500 million—a half-*billion*

TABLE 9

SELECTED MERGERS AND ADVISER FEES, 1982–1987

Year	Merger	Adviser	Fee ($ millions)
1982	U.S. Steel-Marathon Oil	First Boston	$17.4
		Goldman Sachs	10.0
1982	Occidental Petroleum-Cities Service	First Boston	$ 6.1
		Lehman Bros.	6.1
		Goldman Sachs	5.0
		Donaldson Lufkin	1.0
1983	Esmark-Norton Simon	Goldman Sachs	$ 2.5
		Lazard Freres	2.5
		Salomon Bros.	2.5
		Becker-Paribas	1.5
		Oppenheimer	1.5
1984	Chevron-Gulf Oil	Salomon Bros.	$28.2
		Merrill Lynch	18.8
		Morgan Stanley	16.9
1984	Texaco-Getty Oil	Goldman Sachs	$18.5
		Kidder Peabody	15.5
		First Boston	10.8
		Salomon Bros.	na
1984	Mobil Oil-Superior	Morgan Stanley	$12.7
		Goldman Sachs	1.7
1985	Philip Morris-General Foods	First Boston	$10.1
		Goldman Sachs	7.1
		Shearson Lehman	7.1
1985	Allied-Signal	First Boston	$10.0
		Lazard Freres	10.0
1985	R. J. Reynolds-Nabisco	Dillon Read	$ 9.0
		Morgan Stanley	5.0
		Shearson Lehman	5.0
1985	General Motors-Hughes Aircraft	Morgan Stanley	$19.0
		First Boston	15.0
		Salomon Bros.	8.0

Year	Merger	Adviser	Fee ($ millions)
1986	General Electric-RCA	Goldman Sachs	$15.0
		Lazard Freres	12.0
1986	Burroughs-Sperry	First Boston	$ 8.8
		Lazard Freres	7.5
		Wolfensohn	5.0
1986	Macy Department Stores-Associated Dry Goods	Morgan Stanley	$ 6.9
		Goldman Sachs	6.8
		Shearson Lehman	6.8
1987	Unilever-Chesebrough Pond's	Shearson Lehman	$11.0
		Goldman Sachs	8.0
1987	National Amusements-Viacom	Goldman Sachs	$ 8.0
		Merrill Lynch	7.0
1987	Hanson Trust-Kidde	Lazard Freres	$11.8
		Bear Stearns	11.8
		Rothschild	8.0
1987	US Air-Piedmont Airlines	Shearson Lehman	$ 7.2
		First Boston	6.6
1988	Philip Morris-Kraft	Goldman Sachs	$30.0
		Wasserstein-Perella	12.0
		Lazard Freres	3.5
1988	Campeau-Federated Department Stores	First Boston	$18.9
		Wasserstein-Perella	10.0
		Goldman Sachs	17.9
		Shearson Lehman	19.8
		Hellman & Friedman	16.2
1988	BAT-Farmers Group	Goldman Sachs	$12.4
		First Boston	10.8
		Morgan Stanley	9.8
		Conning & Co.	4.1
		Shearson Lehman	2.0
1988	Kodak-Sterling Drug	Morgan Stanley	$28.5
		Shearson Lehman	8.0

Source: "Deals of the Year," *Fortune*, annual.

dollars![24] According to one observer, the real fight was for the fees; R. J. Reynolds was merely the fodder.[25]

Finally, it is important to note that in addition to these fees, corporate deal-mania profits the investment banks in a number of other important ways. It provides a plethora of opportunities for the investment banks' arbitrage operations to profit from temporary stock positions taken in merger and takeover battles—legally in the case of others' deals, illegally in the case of their own. It also churns buying and selling in stocks and bonds traded by the banks.

So win, lose, or draw, the banks get wealthier. Yet the role and growing influence of these marriage brokers poses some troubling questions.

Have the investment banks become perpetual-motion machines demanding a steady (or continually expanding) diet of corporate mergers, acquisitions, and takeovers? Has a self-reinforcing dynamic been unleashed—a dynamic that is inherently insatiable? As one writer, John Brooks, points out, "After a merger has been effected, the same investment banks who promoted it, using the same sales pitches, will be beating the bushes to find someone to take over the company surviving from the first merger. . . . In such a chain letter sequence, intrinsic value need play no real role at all; the mergers operate as pure stock-market plays designed to exploit a current fad."[26]

If this is so, have the banks become something significantly more than mere facilitators of deals? Are they fomenting corporate deal-mania in order to assure a torrent of fees and profits for themselves? And in doing so, are they becoming increasingly detached from economic reality? The similarities with the 1920s are striking. In that earlier era of speculative deal-mania, the "fruits of financial activity were so inviting that bankers began to operate with more and more regard for these fruits and with less and less regard for the effect of such activity upon the businesses involved. The feet of the gentlemen of Wall Street began to leave the hard ground upon which stood factories and shops; these gentlemen began to float higher and higher in a stratospheric region of sheer financial enterprise—a region of reorganizations and mergers and stock split-ups and trading syndicates and super-super-holding companies and investment trusts."[27]

Are the investment banks revolutionizing structure, attitudes, and behavior in the economy at large in a way designed only to fatten their fees at every turn? The expanding, increasingly predominant imperatives (as described by veteran business analyst Jeff Madrick) are these: "If you have a lot of cash, you're vulnerable. If your stock price is low compared to the value of your assets, you're vulnerable. If you're just a very good company in a thriving industry, you're vulnerable. Maybe better to extend your assets a bit too far . . . it might be better to make an acquisition now, better yet a very big acquisition, before you were taken over yourself. A big acquisition puts your money to work, and it's good to borrow plenty as well. More debts make you less attractive."[28] Is this the reemergence of what Frederick Lewis Allen once called a "disorder of irresponsible forces?"

Finally, and most important, does this financier's utopia make economic sense? Is it conducive to better national economic performance? Does it promote productivity, cost efficiency, and technological innovation? Does it contribute to investment in new plants, new products, new manufacturing techniques, and new research and development? Are the corporate marriage brokers the best architects to rely upon in the struggle to reconstruct a competitive world-class economy?

There is a note of irony in this saga: Some leading investment banks are now establishing a brand new line of service. What is it? "Reorganization" advice for collapsing companies, including those that are failing because of uneconomic mergers and acquisitions embarked upon in the past.[29] The service will be provided for a fee, of course.

PART III

THE RESULTS

7

THE MACRO RECORD

They throw cats and dogs together and call them elephants.
—Andrew Carnegie

In this chapter and the next, we reorient our focus. We step back from the merger game. We move away from viewing it in terms of the parochial interests of the players. We leave behind the questions of who plays the game, how they play it, and whether they win or lose.

Instead, we look at the game through the lens of the national interest, and in terms of brute economic fact. We will examine the consequences of the game not for one player or another, but for the country at large. Shorn of PR and stripped of media hype, what does the actual record show? Is the game good for the country? Does corporate deal-mania contribute to better productivity and enhanced efficiency in production? Does it promote new products, new methods of production, and technological advance? Does it contribute to America's efforts to reindustrialize itself and regain world competitive status? Is it laying the foundation for a better, brighter economic future? After the deal is done, after the players tally their wins and losses, and after the enormous egos have exited the stage, has the national interest in better economic performance been advanced? For the players, these questions are irrelevant. But for the nation they are of capital importance. In the final analysis, it is the national well-being that is paramount.

The answer to these questions, provided by a raft of empirical studies, is a resounding "No." The evidence generated from painstaking statistical analyses strongly suggests that merger-mania *undermines* efficiency in production, that it *obstructs* technological advance, and that it *subverts* international competitiveness.

An overview of these findings may be dreary, boring, and repetitive. It is also enlightening—and sobering.

In their monumental study, economists David Ravenscraft and F. M. Scherer examined, in intricate statistical detail, the performance of nearly 6,000 corporate mergers over the 1950–1977 period. They evaluated merged operations according to a variety of economic performance measures, and along a variety of dimensions. They analyzed performance prior to, and following, the consummation of mergers. They compared merged firms' performance with carefully selected control sets of unmerged firms of similar size and in similar markets, industries, and settings. Their findings are devastating for the mergers-promote-performance mythology: The average merger is followed by deteriorating profit performance; the "profitability declines and efficiency losses result[ing] from mergers of the 1960s and early 1970s cast doubt on the widespread applicability of an efficiency theory of merger motives"; there is *no* credible evidence that mergers enhance research and development, and technological innovation; and the adverse performance effects of mergers are responsible to a not insignificant degree for the declining productivity of the American economy. A clear implication, they conclude, is "a skeptical public policy stance toward mergers."[1]

After conducting statistical analyses of corporate mergers and acquisitions for more than a decade, and after an encyclopedic review of other studies, Dennis C. Mueller, professor of economics at the University of Maryland, reports "a surprisingly consistent picture. Whatever the stated or unstated goals of managers are, the mergers they have consummated have on average . . . *not* resulted in economic efficiency."[2] He finds it "impossible to prove from the available empirical evidence that the performance of either the individual merging firms or the economy at large is significantly better as a result of all the mergers that have occurred in this country."[3] He reports: "No support was found for the hypothesis that mergers improve efficiency by consolidating the sales of the acquired companies." He further finds that acquired firms "perform no better if not worse than nonacquired companies in those markets in which each chose to concentrate its sales," and that these failures emerge *following* merger and acquisition.[4] He concludes: "When one looks at the real effects of mergers on operating profitability, growth in sales or market shares, one finds no evidence in the United States that mergers have improved internal efficiency." Indeed, as he views the weight of the empirical evidence, "there is at least as good a chance that slowing down merger activity would increase efficiency in the corporate sector on average."[5]

A Federal Trade Commission staff study, focusing especially on import-affected industries, likewise found that mergers fail to enhance economic performance. The study concluded: "[The] evidence suggests that mergers may *not* be a more significant source of efficiencies in declining industries than in industries generally." In particular, it finds that "the results do *not* indicate that mergers are a particularly efficient form of rationalization."[6]

Nor are acquisition and takeover targets typically broken-down underperformers desperately in need of rejuvenation. According to a detailed analysis of profitability of targets and acquiring firms conducted by Professors Edward Herman and Louis Lowenstein, target firms perform favorably when evaluated against the profitability of the firms seeking to take them over, as well as in comparison with other firms in the same (or similar) industries and operations. "Particularly striking," Lowenstein writes, "is the fact that the targets became substantially more profitable, not less, as the date of the bid approached, not at all what we had been led to expect. What the bidders saw were target managements who were doing well, not poorly, and judging from the target-control companies, the relevant industries were also doing well. Financially speaking, the bidders must have been licking their chops. Here were opportunities to acquire companies that in bottom-line terms were performing better than most, better than their own, and better as time went on." These results, Lowenstein concludes, "cast a serious shadow on the conventional wisdom that takeovers are revitalizing American industry."[7]

Nor is a merger-mania a felicitous instrument for unleashing technological innovation. To the contrary. In a feature cover story, for example, the *Wall Street Journal* reported that the "vast majority of acquisitions of high-technology companies by large corporations have ended in disaster." An important reason, the *Journal* found, is that the "giants' many layers of bureaucracy often paralyze the freewheeling entrepreneurial style typical in the high-tech world."[8] *Forbes* diagnoses the malady as "Bear Hug" disease: "Big companies buy little companies and usually end up destroying the very thing they coveted the small companies for."[9]

The economic infirmities of mergers and acquisitions are graphically shown by their atrocious failure rate. As summarized by *Business Week*: "A half to two-thirds of all mergers don't work; one in three is later undone. In 1985, for every seven acquisitions, there were three divestitures."[10] A McKinsey & Co. analysis of the merger record of 56 large U.S. firms over the years 1972 to 1983 concludes that most (39 of 56) of the firms "that embark on diversification programs fail," and that the danger of failure is greatest for "large unrelated acquisitions."[11] According to management expert Peter Drucker, two mergers out of five are "outright disasters," two "neither live nor die," and one "works."[12] In their statistical work, Ravenscraft and Scherer found "the sell-off rate for acquisitions made in the 1960s and early 1970s to have been somewhere in the range of 19 to 47 percent," and that "the units acquired and later divested were on average in robust good health at the time of their acquisition, but became gravely ill thereafter."[13]

Finally, the failures of mergers are no longer a secret—at least among practical businesspeople in the real world. Prominent business periodicals have been ablaze with articles carrying revealing titles like "Smaller Is Beautiful Now in Manufacturing";[14] "Do

Mergers Really Work?" (the answer: "not very often—which raises serious questions about merger mania");[15] "Big Goes Bust";[16] "Soap and Pastrami Don't Mix";[17] "Splitting Up: The Other Side of Merger Mania";[18] and "Incurable Mergeritis"[19]—hardly inspiring testimonials for the claim that merger-mania benefits the nation's economy. As *Forbes* puts it, the mint that Wall Street's M&A shops are making "may do more to explain the current merger mania than all the blather about synergy and diversification."[20]

If there were a single factor explaining these disappointing findings, it would be the debilitating effect of bureaucracy on human creativity and ingenuity. It is a virus that almost inevitably afflicts giant organizations. As Anthony Downs points out in his definitive study of bureaucracy, large organizational size

> . . . leads to a gradual ossification of operations. Low-level officials find that almost all decisions are delayed for long periods, and merely getting a decision made requires a great deal of persistent effort. Since each proposed action must receive multiple approvals, the probability of its being rejected is quite high. Officials must devote immense efforts to filling out reports, carrying out operationally superfluous procedures, preparing elaborate justifications for past or potential actions, and hosting numerous inspectors. In addition, it becomes extremely difficult to get novel procedures approved. If a proposed action is radically new, it does not fit control processes developed from past experience. Moreover, the need for multiple approval means that one conservative high-ranking official can seriously delay novel procedures by calling for more studies.[21]

Corporate bureaucracy as a concomitant of sheer bigness is not a new phenomenon. In the 1930s, Alfred Sloan (the legendary board chairman of General Motors) ruefully testified to its existence in his corporation:

> In practically all our activities we seem to suffer from the inertia resulting from our great size. It seems to be hard for us to get action when it comes to a matter of putting our ideas across. There are so many people involved and it requires such a tremendous effort to put something new into effect that a new idea is likely to be considered insignificant in comparison with the effort that it takes to put it across. . . . You have no idea how many things come up for consideration in the technical committee and elsewhere that are discussed and agreed upon as to the principle well in advance, but too frequently we fail to put the ideas into effect. . . . Sometimes I am almost forced to the conclusion that General Motors is so large and its inertia so great that it is impossible for us to be leaders.[22]

More recently, H. Ross Perot came up with an almost identical diagnosis. After a brief stint on the GM board of directors, he offered this homely observation: "I come from an environment where, if you see a snake, you kill it. At GM, if you see a snake, the first thing you do is go hire a consultant on snakes. Then you get a committee on snakes, and then you discuss it for a couple of years. The most likely course of action is—nothing. You figure, the snake hasn't bitten anybody yet, so you just let him crawl around on the factory floor. We need to build an environment where the first guy who sees the snake kills it."[23]

Surely, the burden of bureaucracy must be counted as a serious diseconomy of corporate giantism. It is what veteran investment counselor Arthur Burck diagnoses as "the Soviet disease," which is a predictable by-product of merger-induced size. It is a major factor in what the late professor John M. Blair once called "the creative backwardness of bigness."

The empirical evidence has not been kind to the belief in the innovative virtues of corporate mergers, consolidations, and bigness. It is slightly short of ludicrous to embrace the notion of "hierarchical managements sitting in skyscraping offices trying to arrange how brainworkers (who in the future would be most workers) could best use their imaginations."[24]

Is it not more rational, as Tom Peters suggests, to look at the evidence and finally abandon "the most venerated tradition in American economics, or, indeed, the American psyche—that big is good; bigger is better; biggest is best"? Says Peters: "It isn't so. It wasn't so. And it surely won't be so in the future."[25]

8

THE MICRO RECORD

"My name is Ozymandias, King of Kings: Look on my works, ye Mighty, and despair!"
—Percy Bysshe Shelley, "Ozymandias"

The failures and adverse consequences of mergers can be seen in even bolder relief by examining more closely some individual industries and fields. Notable among these are steel, conglomerates, and airlines.

A "big, sprawling, inert giant, whose production operations were improperly coordinated; suffering from a lack of a long-run planning agency; relying on an antiquated system of cost accounting; with an inadequate knowledge of the costs or the relative profitability of the many thousands of items it sold; with production and cost standards generally below those considered everyday practice in other industries; with inadequate knowledge of its domestic markets and no clear appreciation of its opportunities in foreign markets." Thus was the United States Steel Corporation, the nation's largest steel firm, described in the 1930s following an in-depth examination of the firm's affairs conducted by Ford, Bacon & Davis, a management consulting firm. Fifty years later, in 1985, *Business Week* characterized U.S. Steel as "one of America's most hierarchical, bureaucratic managements . . . an inbred, centralized, autocratic bureaucracy that stifles change."

America's steel giants—lumbering, lethargic, more or less continuously collapsing before the onslaught of foreign competition, and incessantly pleading with Washington for bailouts, protection, subsidies, and succor—are to a singular degree the products of eight decades of mergers, acquisitions, and corporate consolidations.

The United States Steel Corporation was created, literally overnight, in 1901. The culmination of a wave of consolidations in the industry begun three years earlier, the firm's formation was guided, financed, and floated by the Jupiter of Wall Street, J. P. Morgan. ("I like competition," Morgan later told a congressional committee, "but I like combination too.") Having earlier instigated consolidations to form the Federal Steel Company, the National Tube Company, and the American Bridge Company, Morgan became captivated by the thought of steel industry consolidation on an even grander scale, as described to him by Charles Schwab (who would later head Bethlehem Steel). At a dinner in late 1900, Schwab glowingly expounded upon "how America could dominate the steel trade of the entire world, if only the industry could be fully integrated for complete efficiency: if inadequate or badly situated plants could be abandoned, new plants could be built in the right places, every unnecessary mile of transportation could be eliminated, and every cost-cutting measure could be taken. Only a single corporation," Schwab said, "which could carry the manufacture of steel through every stage from the mining of ore to the completion of the finished product could accomplish this."[1]

Morgan was convinced. He proceeded to arrange an unprecedented consolidation not only in steel, but in all of American industry. In order to eliminate Andrew Carnegie as an unruly competitive force in the field, enticed by the enormous banking fees of the deal—and, it was claimed, in order to "rationalize" the steel industry and put it on a sounder economic footing—Morgan arranged and floated a combination of eleven major steel firms in early 1901 to create the United States Steel Corporation. But these firms had themselves carried out a number of mergers and acquisitions, so that in all, U.S. Steel was literally a "combination of combinations"—a cumulative consolidation of some 170 formerly independent steel companies, and the nation's first billion-dollar corporation. (Historian Andrew Sinclair points out that it is "hard to imagine what a billion dollars meant at the time. It represented a twenty-fifth of the whole national wealth, more than the combined dividends from the railroads for eight years, and more than the value of all the wheat and barley and cheese and gold and silver and coal produced in 1900 in America.")[2] U.S. Steel's span of operations was truly gargantuan: 213 manufacturing and transportation companies; 41 mines; 1,000 miles of railroad track; and 112 ore vessels. It controlled 66 percent of the nation's steel ingot and castings production, 60 percent of steel rail production, 62 percent of steel structural shapes, 73 percent of coated tin mill products, 68 percent of wire rods, 68 percent of nails, and 83 percent of all seamless tube capacity.[3]

The floating of the U.S. Steel colossus ignited pandemonium in the stock and bond markets, and unleashed wild speculation. "Within a month Steel Common advanced from 38 to 55 and the seven per cent Preferred from 82 to 101. Within a comparatively short time the . . . underwriting syndicate got its money back in cash, plus 200% in dividends. . . . Prices went to the sky. The papers were chock-a-block with tales of sudden fortune that had come to waiters and barbers and clerks."[4] (Subsequent analysis revealed that at least half the stock issued was "water," unbacked by any tangible, physical property.) The profits for the financiers were huge too, amounting to something on the order of $62 million.[5]

In terms of the combine's real economic efficiency, Judge Elbert Gary, appointed the first president of the firm, assured the public that the formation of U.S. Steel would "secure the perfect and permanent harmony in the larger lines of this industry." It would, he said, "result in great benefit to the investor in securities, the consumers, and the workingmen or employees."[6] George W. Perkins, another prominent promoter and director of the corporation, saw it as the salvation of American competitiveness in the global steel markets of the day. Testifying before a Senate committee, Perkins was asked if U.S. Steel's constituent companies would operate more efficiently separately rather than together. "Not as efficient," Perkins replied. "You take ten such companies and go out and compete against Germany. It is self-evident that we could not begin to do it as effectively as with one large company."[7]

Others emulated U.S. Steel's merger-induced giantism. Bethlehem Steel, for example, was incorporated in 1904 as a combination of ten formerly independent steel producers. Bethlehem subsequently acquired thirty-three more steel firms over the period 1914–1945. In fact, as recently as 1958, Bethlehem had yet to expand by building a single new plant in a new location! The genealogy of the other American steel giants—Republic, Jones & Laughlin, Armco, National—is similar. Economist (and now Nobel laureate) George Stigler pointed out in 1950 that not one major American steel company "has been able to add to its relative size as much as 4 percent of the ingot capacity of the industry in 50 years by attracting customers. Every firm that has gained 4 or more percent of the industry's capacity in this half century has done so by merger."[8]

Merger-induced giantism in steel has continued: In 1968, Wheeling Steel (then the industry's 10th largest steel producer) merged with Pittsburgh Steel (at the time the industry's 16th largest firm). In 1971, National Steel (4th largest) acquired Granite City Steel (13th largest). In 1978, Jones & Laughlin Steel (7th largest) was combined with Youngstown Sheet & Tube (8th largest). And in 1984, LTV (the owner of the combined Youngstown–Jones & Laughlin operations, and the nation's 3rd largest steel concern) acquired Republic Steel (4th largest) in a $770 million merger, becoming the 2nd largest steel firm in the country.[9]

And what have eighty years of consolidation, combination, and corporate giantism in American steel produced? Inefficient, unprogressive, hidebound bureaucracies requiring twenty years of government protection from foreign competition and from their own incompetence in order to survive.[10]

Throughout the post-World War II era, Big Steel played the price-wage-price escalation game. It became a powerful engine for cost-push inflation in the economy. It demonstrated a marked aversion to innovation and efficiency, particularly in its failure to adopt (much less to invent) two of the most important technological breakthroughs in steel production in the twentieth century—the oxygen furnace and continuous casting. Big Steel lost export markets abroad and became increasingly vulnerable to import competition at home. In the 1950s, the United States exported about four times as much steel as it imported. By 1968, the situation was reversed by a margin of 8 to 1. The share of foreign competitors (who out-innovated the domestic steel giants) rose steadily from 1 percent in 1956, to 17 percent in 1968, and eventually 27 percent in 1984.

By the 1980s, America's steel giants were generating financial losses of billions of dollars, as well as mass plant closings and job layoffs. They could boast of reducing employment in the industry to fewer than 200,000, the lowest level since records began to be kept in 1933, and far below average employment levels of 450,000 during the 1970s. They were decimating steel-making communities across the country. And in 1986, in spite of its successive mergers with three major steel producers (Jones & Laughlin, Youngstown Sheet & Tube, and Republic Steel), LTV lost $3.3 billion, and then collapsed into bankruptcy.

The cost to the nation of bailing out Big Steel, and protecting it from efficient, innovative foreign competitors through two decades of government import restrictions, has been substantial: It has artificially inflated U.S. steel prices 20 to 40 percent above world levels, handicapped American steel-using firms in world markets, and burdened the American economy with costs variously estimated to be as high as $6.8 billion annually. Obviously, merger-induced giantism has brought about neither production efficiency, nor technological advance, nor international competitiveness. In fact, the opposite seems to be true. While Big Steel has floundered, small "minimill" steel firms have enjoyed spectacular success. They are efficient, sophisticated, and advanced. They are specialized, nonintegrated, and extremely profitable. Their wage rates (with bonuses) are comparable to, or higher than, the wages paid by the steel giants.

These minimill operators bristle with entrepreneurship, efficiency, innovation, and combative competitiveness. Gordon E. Forward, president of Chaparral Steel, a highly successful Texas minimill founded in 1975, epitomizes the breed. "Let's go back to what I think happened at some of the bigger companies in the industry," he says.

> Well, nothing happened. Sure, there was research. But I often thought that those companies had research departments just so the CEOs could say something nice about technology in their annual reports. The companies all put in vice presidents of research. The companies all built important-looking research centers, places with 2,000 people in a spanking new facility out in Connecticut or somewhere, with fountains and lawns and little parks.
>
> Those places were lovely, really nice. But the first time I went into one of them I thought I was entering Forest Lawn [cemetery]. After you spend some time there, you realize you *are* in Forest Lawn. Not because there are no good ideas there, but because the good ideas are dying there all the time.[11]

Gordon Forward shuns formal laboratories. As he sees it, "the lab is the plant." The secret of Chaparral's competitiveness? "In our end of the business, we can't afford to act like fat cats. . . . We constantly chip away the ground we stand on. We have to keep out front all the time. . . . We have built a company that can move fast and that can run full out. We're not the only ones—there are others like us. Nucor does many of the same things. . . . And there's Florida Steel. There are a number of quality mini mills. We are all a little bit different, but we all have to run like hell." And "run like hell" they have, capturing sizable shares of the steel markets in which they compete not only from U.S. steel giants, but from such supposedly invincible foreign producers as Japan, Inc.

Consolidations that further bloat firm size by proliferating the number of anachronistic plants under Big Steel's bureaucratic control are not likely to produce world-class performance. They haven't for eighty years.

They were the *avant-garde* in the salad days of the 1960s. They were the newest of the new. They had abandoned the old ways, they boasted, and were pushing forward the frontiers of organizational "technology." They were catapulting themselves and their firms into the next century. They had seen the future, they said, and it worked. They were the conglomerateurs, who merged scores of firms, in wildly unrelated fields, and then managed them with a vast superstructure of centralized control. They set sail according to the sacred star of "synergy"—the new managerial math by which 2 plus 2 would equal 5. The whole, they believed, would exceed the sum of the parts.

"No creation of the U.S. economy reflects the vigor, imagination, and sheer brass of the 1960s more than the conglomerate corporations," *Business Week* reported in 1968. "Wheeling and dealing with panache and merging with seeming haste all over the lot, they have shattered the cautious business clichés that have prevailed since the Depression." They were shrewd, aggressive, and charismatic. They excited and inspired those around them. They were said to instill entrepreneurial enthusiasm, to pioneer flexible and innovative management techniques, and to employ capital in imaginative new ways. Not committed to, or even knowledgeable in, any particular industry, they were said to possess the kind of free-roving minds able to exploit opportunities wherever and whenever they arose.[12]

These new conglomerates were the darlings of Wall Street. They fomented the kind of action loved by banks and the brokerage houses. As one analyst put it in 1968, the conglomerateurs "make the money move. And when the big money moves, there are fat fees to garner and new investments to make."[13]

But in the end, brute economic reality punctured the hubris and hype of the new conglomerates. The Byzantine, ramshackle superstructures they created eventually turned into organizational nightmares. They ran aground on the reefs of "reverse synergy." They discovered a painful fact of the old math—that once bureaucratic and economic complexities are figured into the equations, 2 plus 2 typically equals 3!

They had, *Forbes* reported, oversold themselves. They "glory in the role of big thinkers and long-range planners. Yet in an uncomfortably large number of acquisitions opportunism has clearly played a larger role than planning."[14] What were billed as the sleek new waves of the future, *Business Week* said, had instead become "multiproduct, multidivisional, multilocational hydras." They were "far too diverse for any one corporate leader to embrace." So they "decentralized into such things as profit centers, strategic business units, and the like." But every profit center, in turn, "had to have a general manager or a divisional president. Corporate headquarters had to have new staff people to whom the divisional people would report." And so, "layer upon layer of management jobs were added to the structure," and the stifling effect of bureaucracy expanded.[15] By their own experience, they discovered (in *Fortune*'s words) that "the cost of complexity outweighs the savings from size."[16]

By their own actions do they stand condemned. What are the brave new conglomerates doing today? *De*-conglomerating! They have discovered that it is "best to divest." They are selling off scores of previously acquired operations. Why? So they can concentrate on what they know best, jettison the rest, and improve their economic and financial performance in the process.

ITT's current president, Rand Araskog, inherited what he describes as "a debt-laden corporation struggling to pay the bills for its many mergers and acquisitions." Summarizing the firm's lackluster performance during the 1970s, one analyst observes that

Harold Geneen, the wizard who masterminded ITT's conglomerate imperialism, "was an absolute disaster as an operating manager. . . . You have only to look at the record—he could acquire companies but not manage them." In a radical reversal of strategy, Araskog divested ITT of businesses with more than $200 million in sales in every year between 1979 and 1983. By the end of 1984, the firm had sold off 69 firms for approximately $2 billion; by 1986, the number of ITT divestitures had reached 100. Says one money manager: "They have had fifteen years of pure junk. I think for the very first time there is a sincere effort to run this thing like a business instead of like an empire."[17]

Gulf & Western (now Paramount) turned itself into what *Fortune* called a "conceptually messy agglutination" of disparate operations. Recognizing this, and in an effort to improve its economic performance, the company in recent years has shed some sixty businesses, ranging from sugar and zinc production to cigar manufacturing and racetracks. "Bigness is not a sign of strength," its current president has said in explaining these divestitures. "In fact, just the opposite is true."[18]

General Mills (Betty Crocker) is now repenting "thirty years of wandering off into fields as diverse as chemicals, luggage and two-man submarines." It has sold off twenty-six businesses in the wake of a loss-ridden conglomerate acquisition spree that included restaurants, Play Doh, Izod sportswear, Monet jewelry, Kenner toys, and Parker Brothers games. (Of the bureaucratic morass created by General Mills in the toy business, one marketing manager recalls a "never-ending procession to General Mills. We started to think we were in the presentation business rather than the toy business.") Informed analysts now conclude that General Mills "learned the hard way that it was easier to buy businesses it knew little about than to manage them."[19]

Big Oil has struggled to extricate itself from a series of disastrous forays into conglomerate expansionism. Flush with cash in the 1970s, *Forbes* points out, "oil companies handled the money badly, overpaying for fashionable diversification and overdosing on overhead. Mobil and Exxon and Chevron, Standard Oil and Atlantic

Richfield wasted much of the fruits of the now vanished prosperity in buying into businesses their managements knew nothing about. Intoxicated with profits, they became victims of hubris." They dissipated their stockholders' funds "in overpriced and badly conceived diversification."[20] By the 1980s, alas, ARCO had disposed of its ill-fated acquisition of Anaconda Minerals, absorbing a $785 million writedown. Mobil Oil had finally found a buyer for its perennially money-losing albatross, the ill-fated Montgomery Ward retailing subsidiary. Exxon had written off hundreds of millions of dollars of failed investments in Reliance Electric—dubbed by *Fortune* "Exxon's $600 Million Mistake"—and in office equipment systems. Amoco had spun off Cyprus Mines, a copper producer. And Schlumberger had sold Fairchild Semiconductor, absorbing a $200 million writeoff in this failed conglomerate acquisition.

Big Steel's conglomerate merger record is just as embarrassing. Armco Steel's acquisition of insurance operations in the early 1980s has, to date, produced cumulative financial losses for the firm in excess of a half-billion dollars. National Steel's diversification into oil, pharmaceuticals distribution, and five-and-dime retailing (Ben Franklin stores) is foundering. And U.S. Steel has divested chemical operations that languished under the firm's bureaucratic tutelage.

The fact of the matter is that conglomerate merger-mania has been a colossal flop. Perhaps the postmortem has been delivered by Donald P. Jacobs, dean of the Kellogg School of Management at Northwestern University. Reflecting on recent developments, he observes that "the thinking used to be that once a conglomerate was put together, the whole was more valuable than the parts. Now the parts seem to be more valuable than the whole." Chastened Armco Steel president Robert E. Boni is more blunt: "There are various reasons for diversification, and most are invalid."

He is intense but aloof, a devoted marathon runner and nutritionist, who projects an arresting mien at once distant and concentrated. He is a deft financier, a demanding boss—and the scourge of airline unions and pilots. He is Frank Lorenzo. In 1969, three years out of the Harvard Business School and 29 years old, Lorenzo incorporated an aircraft leasing business called Jet Capital. Three years later, he was elected president of Texas International Airlines—a tiny, ailing Texas airline known as Tree Top Airways—after devising a plan to rescue the firm from insolvency. Struggling to expand his operation, Lorenzo asked the Civil Aeronautics Board for permission to slash fares in order to build business. Early in 1977, the deregulation-minded CAB granted Texas International permission to offer what the carrier called Peanut Fares, half-price tickets on lightly traveled routes.

Although Texas International was soon one of the fastest growing airlines in the country, it was too small for Lorenzo's ambitions. He contrived a plan to use leverage—borrowed money—to take over a major carrier. In 1978 he went after National Airlines, a major carrier based in Miami. Although he was eventually outbid by Pan Am, he pocketed a profit of $46 million when he sold the National stock he had acquired in the effort.

In 1980, Lorenzo established New York Air, a nonunion, low-cost carrier created to compete with Eastern Airlines' New York to Washington shuttle service. In the same year, Lorenzo created the Texas Air Corporation as a holding company, with controlling interests in Texas International, New York Air, and Lorenzo's expanding empire. (In 1980, one of Lorenzo's lieutenants, Donald C. Burr, left Texas International to found People Express, one of the first major new upstarts to enter the newly deregulated airline field.) In early 1981, his appetite growing, Lorenzo went after Continental Airlines, the nation's 10th largest air carrier at the time. The Continental takeover was brutal; when it became clear that Lorenzo had won, Continental's chief executive committed suicide.

But Lorenzo still wasn't finished. He now dreamed of building an even bigger "mega-carrier." Following a failed effort to acquire TWA (which he lost to corporate raider Carl Icahn), Lorenzo set his sights on Eastern Airlines. In early 1986 he succeeded, paying $640 million to acquire Eastern. Later that year he acquired People Express for $450 million from his former colleague Donald Burr, who in turn had just acquired Frontier Airlines. In addition to these major carriers, Lorenzo bought a number of smaller commuter lines, including Rocky Mountain Air, Britt Airways, Bar Harbor Airways, and Provincetown-Boston Airlines. Lorenzo also bought Braniff's Latin American routes. In the single year 1986–1987, Lorenzo's air fleet had grown by more than threefold (from 175 to 602 planes); his market share had risen from 7 to 20 percent; and his work force had exploded from 15,500 to 63,000 employees.

Now, at last, Frank Lorenzo's dream was a reality. Through mergers and consolidations, he had turned a regional Texas carrier into the free world's largest airline. From Texas International in 1972, with assets of $15 million and revenues of $70 million, Lorenzo now stood astride a true mega-carrier, with assets of $8 billion and $4.4 billion in annual revenues. He controlled fully a fifth of the U.S. air market, east to west and north to south; his planes flew to 225 cities across the nation and around the world.[21]

For Lorenzo, the name of the game seemed to be size—size for size's sake, not quality. In an in-depth 1987 analysis of Lorenzo's empire, *Barron's* reported that the "quintessential Continental Airlines experience recently has been to arrive at the wrong terminal building at Newark International Airport for a delayed Continental flight on a People Express plane serving an in-flight snack in New York Air's 'Flying Nosh' bags under the care of green flight attendants who could barely get through the preflight safety speech without a script." Not quite the "friendly skies," the magazine quipped.[22]

These airline industry events poignantly demonstrate the adverse economic consequences that result when anticompetitive mergers between rivals in the same field are allowed to proliferate without restraint. It shows how a naive government policy of laissez-faire toward mergers can subvert the gains from deregulation. It also illustrates how, in the absence of an effective antimerger policy, corporate consolidations can substitute oligopoly and monopoly control for government control.

Beginning in 1938 and for forty years thereafter, the Civil Aeronautics Board (CAB) administered a government-created, government-maintained, government-enforced cartel of U.S. air service. It controlled the number of carriers allowed to operate, the routes they could fly, the specific city points they were permitted to serve, and the fares they were required to charge. Under the CAB's aegis, the industry became what former FTC chairman Lewis Engman called a "federal protectorate, living in a cozy world of cost-plus, safely protected from the ugly specters of competition, efficiency, and innovation." CAB regulation and suppression of competition produced a harvest of substandard performance: New entry was foreclosed to even the safest of potential new entrants; air routes were frozen; smaller cities suffered declining service; fares were inflated far above competitive levels; and carriers channeled their competitive energies into costly, inefficient nonprice rivalry.[23]

In 1978, confronted with an accumulating body of persuasive evidence, Congress and the Carter administration opted for competition in the industry. While the government would retain responsibility for air safety, the competitive market would be relied on to determine how many carriers would fly what routes, and at what fares. Initial results were promising: The number of scheduled carriers nearly tripled; fares (in inflation-adjusted terms) declined 13 percent on average; productivity improved by an estimated 80 percent, with cumulative cost savings of as much as $10 billion; and air travel expanded at significantly higher annual rates, as larger numbers of people found it increasingly affordable.

But these benefits would be obtained only so long as the industry remained competitively structured—that is, only so long as the government vigilantly guarded against anticompetitive mergers and consolidations between competing carriers. Instead, the Reagan administration abdicated its antitrust responsibilities and cheerfully presided over the most voracious merger and acquisition movement in the industry's history.[24] The pivotal acquisition occurred in 1985, when the Reagan administration approved United's $750 million purchase of Pan Am's trans-Pacific air routes. Because only three American carriers (Pan Am, United, and Northwest) served these routes, the merger reduced the number of American competitors from three to two. By linking United's extensive domestic operations to Pan Am's routes, the merger greatly enhanced United's ability to feed domestic passengers into its trans-Pacific flights.

In response, and in order to link a more extensive domestic system to its international routes, Northwest acquired Republic Airlines. This $884 million merger marked a consolidation between the nation's 7th and 9th largest carriers, creating the nation's 3rd largest airline. The administration approved the merger despite evidence that the combination would control nearly 80 percent of the Minneapolis market; that (according to the Justice Department) it could have "substantial anticompetitive effects" in as many as 86 domestic route markets; and that by lessening competition, the Northwest-Republic merger would inflate airfares, possibly by as much as $64 million annually.

With the Reagan administration's blessings, the merger game quickly consumed the remainder of the industry. After having acquired Continental Airlines in 1982, Texas Air's Frank Lorenzo was permitted to acquire Eastern Airlines and People Express (after People Express had acquired Frontier Airlines). As a result, Texas Air quickly became the free world's largest air carrier. It dominated the entire eastern seaboard, from Boston, New York, and Washington to Charlotte and Miami; and it combined a large network of Latin American routes (which Eastern acquired from Pan Am) with Texas Air's extensive domestic flight system. The firm's imperialism prompted one cynic to remark that only the U.S. Air Force remained for Frank Lorenzo to conquer. Lorenzo was not unique, however. In an especially anticompetitive deal, TWA was allowed to acquire Ozark Airlines, despite the fact that the two carriers were the largest competitors in the St. Louis market; that TWA accounted for 57 percent, and Ozark for 27 percent of the St. Louis market; and that the combined carrier would control 18 of the 28 nonstop routes on which the two formerly competed.

Merger-mania next swept the western United States. Delta Airlines, the nation's 6th largest carrier, was permitted to acquire Western Airlines, the nation's 9th largest carrier, in a merger valued at $860 million. US Air was allowed to buy Pacific Southwestern Airlines (PSA)—a $400 million merger combining US Air's service to 83 airports (mostly in the eastern United States) with PSA's 29-airport route system (mostly on the West Coast), and creating the nation's 7th largest carrier at the time. And American Airlines was permitted to acquire AirCal in a $225 million merger triggered in important part by Delta's purchase of Western.

In 1987, US Air acquired Piedmont Airlines—one of the fastest-growing, most profitable, and most competitive national carriers to emerge following deregulation. The Reagan administration approved this $1.6 billion merger despite the fact that the two carriers operated out of 57 of the same airports and competed directly on routes between 21 identical city pairs. In all, in a brief two-year period the Reagan administration sanctioned some 26 airline mergers involving upward of 70 percent of the industry's entire capacity. Guided by a radical laissez-faire ideology, it permitted the creation of a highly concentrated industry structure, wherein the collective share of the 10 largest carriers has escalated sharply from 75 percent in 1984 to 95 percent in 1988.

The anticompetitive impact of the administration's benign neglect is especially evident in regional air markets and individual cities. For example, St. Louis was served by five carriers prior to deregulation in 1978; nine additional carriers entered the St. Louis market after 1978. Today, however, following TWA's acquisition of Ozark, TWA controls 82 percent of St. Louis air passenger traffic. As Table 10 shows, the problem of extremely high, anticompetitive concentration is replicated in major cities across the nation. At 22 of the nation's major airports, one carrier now controls over 50 percent of the air traffic; at 9 of them, a single carrier controls more than 75 percent.[25]

Predictably, this noncompetitive industry structure is now producing noncompetitive performance. "The present situation at hub airports is intolerable," says Senator Jack Danforth. "Deregulation was supposed to create competition," Congressman Wendell Ford complains. Instead, he says, the traveling public is now "looking down the barrel of a gun." Air fares are rising, while the quality of service deteriorates. After acquiring Ozark, for example, TWA cut

TABLE 10

TRENDS IN REGIONAL AIRPORT DOMINATION, 1977–1987

Airport	Dominant Carrier	Market Share of Largest Carrier 1977	1987
Baltimore/Washington	US Air	25%	60%
Cincinnati	Delta	35	68
Detroit	Northwest	21	65
Houston	Continental	20	72
Memphis	Northwest	40	87
Minneapolis	Northwest	46	82
Nashville	American	28	60
Pittsburgh	US Air	44	83
St. Louis	TWA	39	82
Salt Lake City	Delta	40	75

Source: *Consumer Reports,* June 1988.

40 flights out of St. Louis, and raised fares by as much as 33 percent.[26] Northwest cut the number of departures from Minneapolis by nearly 15 percent following its acquisition of Republic. Chart 2 shows that at 18 hubs where a single airline controls 50 percent or more of the traffic, originating passengers now pay significantly higher fares—in some cases over 50 percent more—compared to standard industry fare levels. As dominant carriers carve up the country into regional monopolies, the flying public pays more and more for less and less.

Thus, mergers have proliferated, concentration has climbed, and performance is falling. As the *Wall Street Journal* puts it, "the airlines have used the nation's air route system like a giant chess board in the sky, moving in and out of markets" in order to avoid competition.[27] "The onus is heavily on the airlines," says William F. Buckley, Jr. "De facto, they exercise near-monopoly privileges and abuse an important percentage of the traveling public."[28]

Yet the blame lies not with deregulation, but in the Reagan

CHART 2

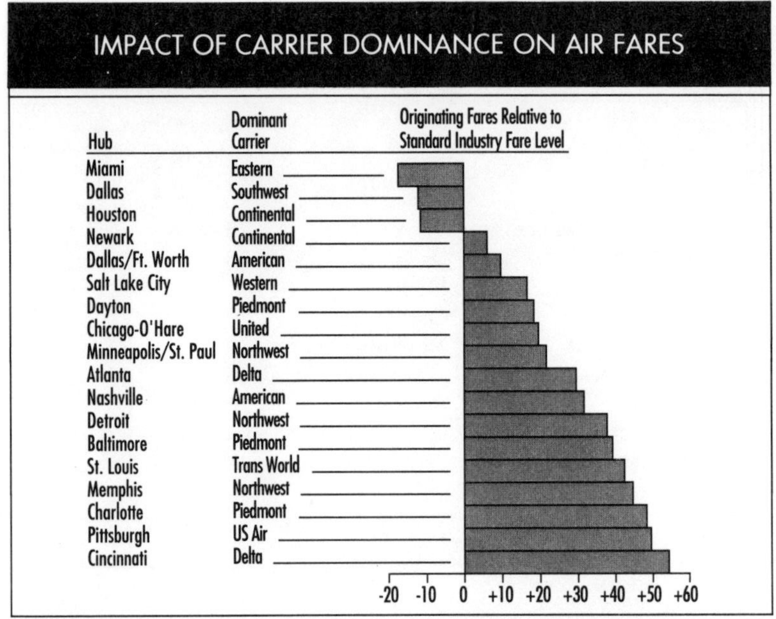

Note: Hubs showns are those where the largest carrier emplanes 50% or more of all air passengers.
Source: Airline Economics, Inc., *Blue Chip Airline Financial Indictors*, Fall 1988.

administration's failure to arrest anticompetitive merger trends. Ironically, this has precipitated a cacophony of cries for reregulation of the airline industry[29]—which, if it comes to pass, will mean that the Reagan administration will have subverted the very deregulation program it professed to cherish.

No purpose is served by a proliferation of such case studies. The scribbler who, a hundred years hence, will write the definitive treatise on the decline and fall of industrial empires will have more than enough empirical evidence.

per share; their shares subsequently
ent increase! The leveraged buyout of
participants to triple their investment,
million. A group of investors bought
re; six months later the firm was sold
any of Japan at a price of $17.25 per
Top executives and investment banks
for 25 cents a share; when later taken
ched $11 each—a 4,300 percent gain.
ass Containers, Inc., Mr. Simon resold
acquired for a mere 19 cents a share—
t![8]

ked in, pushed out, and sucked back
profit for the professionals adept at
lion. In the case of Amstar (a sugar
nanagement together with investment
n equity in the first buyout of the firm
rty-eight months later, in another sale
stood to quadruple their $60 million
s case, the original stockholders parted
re—stock that now is worth more than

d small have been slaughtered by deal-
emiums, high debt-equity ratios, and
harges combine to destroy the quality
hold. In the aftermath of the buyout
ple, the firm's outstanding long-term
200 for every $1,000 in face value. As
's takeover of Federated Department
more than 17 percent in value. RJR-
n estimated $800 million as a result of
by Kohlberg Kravis Roberts. (In this
politan Life, filed suit against RJR after
e firm drop by some $40 million. ITT
R, for the same reason.) In fact, the
eal knocked down bond prices for a

9
THE SMALL INVESTOR

Some day I'm goin' to go out an' hang ivry damn widow and orphan between th' rollin' mills an' th' foundlin's' home. If it wasn't f'r thim rapayshus craychures, they'd be no boodle annywhere.

—Mr. Dooley

Today, it is no longer widows and orphans but the "small investors" who are paraded about as the real beneficiaries of the merger game. It is ostensibly for them that billion-dollar deals are contrived and launched. It is purportedly on their behalf that raiders, managers, bankers, and buyout artists selflessly hurl themselves into financial combat. But here, as elsewhere, the reality is otherwise. Far from benefitting, small investors—and at times large ones, too—lose in a number of important ways.

First, the stock value of acquisitive firms typically *falls* an average 1 to 7 percent in the first year, and a cumulative 16 percent over the three years following a corporate takeover.[1] In their analysis of acquiring firms completing takeovers during the years 1976 to 1981, Professors Magenheim and Mueller found the adverse stock price effects of takeovers to be even worse—cumulative total declines relative to premerger trends of 27 to 42 percent. After three years, they calculate, shareholders are "significantly worse off" than they would have been had their firms refrained from engaging in takeovers and acquisitions.[2] Even the most doctrinaire defenders of takeovers cannot evade this uncomfortable fact. Jensen and Ruback, who otherwise extol the virtues of deal-mania, confess that these stock price declines "are unsettling because they are inconsistent with market efficiency and suggest that changes in stock price during takeovers overestimate the future efficiency gains from mergers."[3]

Second, these declines typically cancel out any gains in the stock value of target firms at the time of takeover. Murray Weidenbaum, President Reagan's first chairman of the Council of Economic Advisers, finds in his studies that "the data do not support the notion that the owners of acquiring firms generally benefit from takeovers." Instead, he concludes, the "available evidence of aggregate returns further suggests that acquiring firms' losses on average are large enough to completely offset the gains made by owners of the target firms."[4] That is, considered as a group, stockholders typically lose.

Third, professional arbitrageurs frequently are the first to load up on the stock of likely takeover target firms at the relatively low prices that prevail before the bidding frenzy drives stock prices through the ceiling. As a result, a large share of the substantial takeover premiums are cornered by "arbs" on Wall Street, not the small investors on Main Street. As John Brooks points out, advocates of mergers and acquisitions "argue that they are advantageous to stockholders because of the premium, often very large, that is paid by the acquirer. But in practice, most of that profit almost always goes to arbitrageurs."[5] Other "prescient" persons also do quite well. The stock of target companies exhibits abnormal trading and price gains more than three weeks before deals are disclosed to the public.[6] Those able to gorge themselves on such stocks at bargain prices—long before impending deals are announced—benefit handsomely. It is a profitable inside trading loop safely removed from the pockets of small investors.

Fourth, leveraged buyouts are also no boon for small investors. When publicly held firms are bought out and "taken private" by an elite coterie of insiders, only to be later sold back to the public

an average price of 88 cent
rose to $15.50—a 1,661 perc
Motel 6 permitted the inside
from $132 million to $332
Dunlop Tire for $2.50 a sha
to Sumitomo Rubber Comp
share—a 600 percent gain.[7]
bought out Harley-Davidson
public again, their shares fe
And in the case of Anchor G
stock for $20.50 that he had
a tidy gain of 10,689 percen

Small investors can be suc
in again, with considerable
playing this financial accor
refiner, appropriately), the r
banks turned their $55 millic
into a $240 million profit. Fo
of the firm, the same group
investment once again. In thi
with their stock for $47 a sha
twice that much.[9]

Fifth, bondholders large an
mania, as high takeover pr
astronomical fixed interest c
and value of the bonds they
of Colt Industries, for exam
bonds plunged as much as $
a result of Robert Campeau
Stores, Federated's bonds fel
Nabisco bonds plummeted a
that firm's leveraged buyout
case, one bondholder, Metro
seeing its bondholdings in th
has also filed suit against R
reverberations of the RJR d

9

THE SMALL INVESTOR

Some day I'm goin' to go out an' hang ivry damn widow and orphan between th' rollin' mills an' th' foundlin's' home. If it wasn't f'r thim rapayshus craychures, they'd be no boodle annywhere.

—Mr. Dooley

Today, it is no longer widows and orphans but the "small investors" who are paraded about as the real beneficiaries of the merger game. It is ostensibly for them that billion-dollar deals are contrived and launched. It is purportedly on their behalf that raiders, managers, bankers, and buyout artists selflessly hurl themselves into financial combat. But here, as elsewhere, the reality is otherwise. Far from benefitting, small investors—and at times large ones, too—lose in a number of important ways.

First, the stock value of acquisitive firms typically *falls* an average 1 to 7 percent in the first year, and a cumulative 16 percent over the three years following a corporate takeover.[1] In their analysis of acquiring firms completing takeovers during the years 1976 to 1981, Professors Magenheim and Mueller found the adverse stock price effects of takeovers to be even worse—cumulative total declines relative to premerger trends of 27 to 42 percent. After three years, they calculate, shareholders are "significantly worse off" than they would have been had their firms refrained from engaging in takeovers and acquisitions.[2] Even the most doctrinaire defenders of takeovers cannot evade this uncomfortable fact. Jensen and Ruback, who otherwise extol the virtues of deal-mania, confess that these stock price declines "are unsettling because they are inconsistent with market efficiency and suggest that changes in stock price during takeovers overestimate the future efficiency gains from mergers."[3]

Second, these declines typically cancel out any gains in the stock value of target firms at the time of takeover. Murray Weidenbaum, President Reagan's first chairman of the Council of Economic Advisers, finds in his studies that "the data do not support the notion that the owners of acquiring firms generally benefit from takeovers." Instead, he concludes, the "available evidence of aggregate returns further suggests that acquiring firms' losses on average are large enough to completely offset the gains made by owners of the target firms."[4] That is, considered as a group, stockholders typically lose.

Third, professional arbitrageurs frequently are the first to load up on the stock of likely takeover target firms at the relatively low prices that prevail before the bidding frenzy drives stock prices through the ceiling. As a result, a large share of the substantial takeover premiums are cornered by "arbs" on Wall Street, not the small investors on Main Street. As John Brooks points out, advocates of mergers and acquisitions "argue that they are advantageous to stockholders because of the premium, often very large, that is paid by the acquirer. But in practice, most of that profit almost always goes to arbitrageurs."[5] Other "prescient" persons also do quite well. The stock of target companies exhibits abnormal trading and price gains more than three weeks before deals are disclosed to the public.[6] Those able to gorge themselves on such stocks at bargain prices—long before impending deals are announced—benefit handsomely. It is a profitable inside trading loop safely removed from the pockets of small investors.

Fourth, leveraged buyouts are also no boon for small investors. When publicly held firms are bought out and "taken private" by an elite coterie of insiders, only to be later sold back to the public

TABLE 11

CHANGES IN MARKET VALUE FOR SELECTED LBO DEALS

Company	Buyout Value Paid ($ millions)	Value When Later Taken Public or Sold ($ millions)	Percent Increase
Beatrice	$6,200	$8,800–10,800*	42–74
Blue Bell	70	792	1031
Dr. Pepper	650	866	33
Leslie Fay	58	360	521
Lily Tulip	180	326	81
Metromedia	1,100	6,500*	490
Fred Meyer	420	900*	114
SFN	450	1,100*	144
Uniroyal	900	1,400*	55

* Estimated.
Source: U.S. Congress, House, Subcommittee on Oversight and Investigations of the Committee on Energy and Commerce, *Committee Print: Leveraged Buyouts and the Pot of Gold: Trends, Public Policy and Case Studies,* 100th Cong., 1st Sess., 1987, pp. 28–29.

with handsome gains, the small investor seldom shares in the bonanza. Table 11 depicts the value received by the original stockholders in nine buyouts, and the vastly higher value captured by the participants in the buyout when the operations were subsequently sold off. The differences, which average a spectacular 281 percent for the deals shown in Table 11, do not accrue to the small investors. Indeed, small investors part with stock shares that are worth far more than what they receive for them, goaded by "fairness letters" issued by investment banks which, in turn, have a sizable monetary stake in seeing the deal (and their fees) materialize.

The gains to the inside players who contrive these deals—gains that also bypass the small investor—are unbelievable: Managers of Western Auto, for example, together with former Treasury Secretary William E. Simon's buyout firm, bought the firm's stock at an average price of 88 cents per share; their shares subsequently rose to $15.50—a 1,661 percent increase! The leveraged buyout of Motel 6 permitted the inside participants to triple their investment, from $132 million to $332 million. A group of investors bought Dunlop Tire for $2.50 a share; six months later the firm was sold to Sumitomo Rubber Company of Japan at a price of $17.25 per share—a 600 percent gain.[7] Top executives and investment banks bought out Harley-Davidson for 25 cents a share; when later taken public again, their shares fetched $11 each—a 4,300 percent gain. And in the case of Anchor Glass Containers, Inc., Mr. Simon resold stock for $20.50 that he had acquired for a mere 19 cents a share—a tidy gain of 10,689 percent![8]

Small investors can be sucked in, pushed out, and sucked back in again, with considerable profit for the professionals adept at playing this financial accordion. In the case of Amstar (a sugar refiner, appropriately), the management together with investment banks turned their $55 million equity in the first buyout of the firm into a $240 million profit. Forty-eight months later, in another sale of the firm, the same group stood to quadruple their $60 million investment once again. In this case, the original stockholders parted with their stock for $47 a share—stock that now is worth more than twice that much.[9]

Fifth, bondholders large and small have been slaughtered by dealmania, as high takeover premiums, high debt-equity ratios, and astronomical fixed interest charges combine to destroy the quality and value of the bonds they hold. In the aftermath of the buyout of Colt Industries, for example, the firm's outstanding long-term bonds plunged as much as $200 for every $1,000 in face value. As a result of Robert Campeau's takeover of Federated Department Stores, Federated's bonds fell more than 17 percent in value. RJR-Nabisco bonds plummeted an estimated $800 million as a result of that firm's leveraged buyout by Kohlberg Kravis Roberts. (In this case, one bondholder, Metropolitan Life, filed suit against RJR after seeing its bondholdings in the firm drop by some $40 million. ITT has also filed suit against RJR, for the same reason.) In fact, the reverberations of the RJR deal knocked down bond prices for a host of consumer goods firms, including Ralston Purina, Procter & Gamble, and Sara Lee. In all, then, bondholders—who are also investors—are estimated to have lost tens of billions of dollars from the corporate deal-mania of the 1980s.[10]

Sixth, the lion's share of the multibillion-dollar booty is primarily captured not by small investors on Main Street, but by the professional inside players on Wall Street—investment banks, corporate executives, arbitrageurs, and (at times) criminally knowledgeable inside traders.

Consider the multibillion-dollar Time-Warner consolidation as originally contemplated: Warner chief executive officer Steven J. Ross expected to receive close to $50 million by exercising his stock option rights. In addition, several top Warner executives could receive $10 to $15 million each by exercising their holdings of Warner stock options. Time chairman J. Richard Munro, who would serve as co-chief executive of Time-Warner, would receive at least $1.4 million in annual salary and bonus each year. If he retired before May 1990, he would get $4.2 million in deferred compensation, and could draw a base salary of $750,000 annually as chairman of the merged firms' executive committee. Time president N. J. Nicholas, Jr., who initially would be president of Time-Warner and its sole chief executive after five years, would receive an annual salary and bonus of at least $1.3 million. At the conclusion of his term as chief executive, he would receive $750,000 annually for five years. In addition to all of the foregoing, sources expected the merged firm to raise the salaries of many Time managers to bring them "in line" with the richer compensation structure at Warner—all, ostensibly, in order to enhance American competitiveness in world markets.[11]

In fact, golden parachutes seem to have facilitated top management's accommodation to deal-mania. In the Allied-Signal consolidation, for example, top executives of the firms were estimated to have garnered at least $50 million in a cornucopia of cash, stock giveaways, stock options, and other benefits.[12] William Agee pocketed $4 million after agreeing to sell Bendix to Allied Corporation in 1983.[13] When Pantry Pride acquired Revlon in 1985, Revlon chairman Michel Bergerac was enriched to the tune of $35 million, including $7 million in cash payments and $21 million in stock and stock options.[14] As *Fortune* points out, the personal gain to top management in these deals "propels them to the outer limits of the known universe for executive compensation."[15]

Alas, milking the small investor is nothing new. Instead, it is an enduring and probably integral part of the merger and acquisition game. Examining the four major merger movements in the United States over the ninety-year period 1897–1987, Professors DuBoff and Herman find each commonly marked by "significant degrees of misinformation, manipulation, the outcropping of fads, euphoria and speculation." They find "a consistent historical record that the merger gains of promoters, investment bankers, and corporate insiders have been 'more unequivocal' than those of the shareholders." Of the turn-of-the-century merger movement, they conclude that "the function of the publicity supplied to investors was not to elucidate but to sell, and it was so misleading as to constitute, in effect, a disinformation campaign."

Of the 1920s merger movement, DuBoff and Herman report: "Many of the holding company structures and investment companies of the 1920s were organized to take advantage of bull market psychology and to feed the demands of the extensive security selling apparatus built up in the late 1920s. Hard sell tactics and misrepresentation on a very large scale characterized this market. The financial establishment encouraged the new army of investors to believe that everyone could get rich in the ever-upward market of the New Era." (Of this speculative age, Frederick Lewis Allen wrote that the New York Stock Exchange might well have been called the Association for Improving the Condition of the Rich.)[16]

As for the "Go-Go" conglomerate merger craze of the 1960s, DuBoff and Herman find the "movement was initiated and promoted mainly by conglomerate entrepreneurs, with investment bankers, commercial bankers, and the brokerage community serving more as advisers, finders, and cooperative lenders and security salespeople. The bankers and brokers were important gainers. . . . The inside managers-promoters were major winners. . . . [But the] shareholders of the acquiring firms, as we have seen, were on average nongainers."[17]

The evidence is persuasive and the conclusion plausible: Mergermania is now—and has long been—a financial shell game played to enrich an elite band of greed merchants on Wall Street. The gains accruing to the small investor seem to be incidental, at best.

10

THE CASINO SOCIETY

Soon fades the spell, soon comes the night;
Say will it not be then the same,
Whether we played the black or white,
Whether we lost or won the game?
—Macaulay

What goes around, comes around.

Hebrew National Kosher Foods, Inc., was a relatively insignificant privately held company that had been selling its line of kosher salami, frankfurters, corned beef, and other delicatessen products for eighty years. Run by Isadore Pinckowitz (a Rumanian butcher who peddled meat from the back of a horse-drawn wagon when he first came to the United States) and by his descendants, the company was a huge financial success. In 1968, Hebrew National was sold to Houston-based Riviana Foods, Inc., which saw in the company not just salami but a chance to break out of the low-profile commodity rice business. Eight years later, Riviana (including Hebrew National) was acquired by Colgate-Palmolive. "It was not a happy fit," *Forbes* reports. "A bunch of Madison Avenue soap salesmen suddenly found themselves dealing in kosher food."[1] When Colgate-Palmolive realized that pastrami and soap don't mix, it decided to fire the CEO who had conceived the diversification strategy. Colgate would be "restructured," and Hebrew National would be sold. To whom? Why, the original owners, of course.

Today, *Forbes* finds, "Hebrew National is a private company again and run like one. [Its president] watches each market carefully so that his product is priced competitively. He visits the factory and tastes its product several times a week. Time formerly wasted on meeting corporate reporting requirements can be devoted to minding the store."[2] The results speak for themselves: Since regaining its independence, the company has doubled in size and is profitable once again. The story, *Forbes* concludes, illustrates "that a lot of today's made-in-heaven mergers and takeovers are at least as ill-matched as this one was—profitable only for the brokers and deal-makers,"[3] who have helped convert the American economy into a casino society.

The battle for corporate control is a zero-sum game. It does not create new assets; it only rearranges them. It does not increase the size of the pie; it merely rearranges the slices. In real terms, it does not add to the wealth of a nation; it simply redistributes existing wealth. It is an exercise in paper entrepreneurialism.

Paper entrepreneurialism—that is, asset-trading—has tantalizing attractions. "Faced with the alternatives of investing corporate earnings in new plant, equipment, or research (risky propositions whose payoffs are likely to be in the distant future)," says Robert B. Reich, "corporate managers instead see considerable attraction in buying profitable, well-run companies with established market positions."[4] Merger, buyout, and takeover artists speak of synergy, making the whole greater than the sum of its parts. They point to high underlying values of the acquired assets relative to their market price, values waiting to be enhanced by superior management. But the facts belie these claims.

Improvements in productivity often depend on investment strategies geared to the long term, Reich told a congressional committee:

> Research aimed at developing fundamentally new technologies is apt to be slow, yielding little or no profit for many years. The development of the internal combustion engine, electronics, xerography, and semiconductors each depended on a quarter century or more of trial and error. Commercialization often requires the development of large scale production facilities, distribution and sales networks, and quality control systems. All this necessitates a willingness to invest now for greater return in the more distant future.[5]

One generation must plant trees, says a Chinese proverb, if the next is to enjoy their fruit.

Corporate asset-rearrangers, however, typically insist on shorter-term payoffs. They are not prepared to wait. They want immediate returns on their investment, even at the expense of higher returns in the future. So do portfolio managers of mutual funds, pension funds, and insurance companies, which often move in and out of large positions with more regard to high paper yields in the proximate future than concern for the fundamental strengths of a corporate enterprise. Security analysts and brokers too are obsessed with a corporation's price-earnings multiples this year and next; they exhibit only mild interest in the corporation's status five or ten years from now. Budget Director Richard Darman calls this the "now-now-ism" affliction—a "shorthand label for our collective shortsightedness, our obsession with the here and now, our reluctance to address the future." The entire nation, he recently told a banquet audience, is like the spoiled child in the 1950s commercial who screams: "I want my Maypo! I want it NOW." No wonder, said Darman, Wall Street institutions "feel obliged to chase near-term financial gains."

This short-term balance sheet mentality has untoward consequences. As the MIT Commission on Industrial Productivity points out, managers are preoccupied by "the fear that development and investment policies oriented toward the long term will be undervalued by the market and leave their firm vulnerable to takeover."[6] This fear also militates against investment in the kind of R&D that may produce technological breakthroughs a decade from now. It downgrades the importance of investing in plant construction and modernization that may reduce costs and improve quality. At the same time, it enhances the incentives to play it safe by buying rather than building. After all, a bird in the hand is worth two in the bush. This choice of corporate strategy is not costless, and experience provides ample evidence to prove it.

In 1960, Gulf & Western Corporation was an obscure car bumper company that did not rank among the nation's 200 largest industrial concerns. Just eight years later, however, Gulf & Western (satirized in a Mel Brooks movie as Engulf & Devour) was a colossus—the 34th largest industrial firm in the country, the 17th largest in terms of consolidated assets.

The company's meteoric rise was not the fruit of patiently planned long-term investment or irresistible product innovations. Instead, it was bought through mergers and acquisitions. During the 1960s, Gulf & Western's acquisitions included 33 wholesalers of automotive parts; manufacturers of automobile pistons and parking-brake levers; a full-line integrated producer of zinc; a manufacturer of fittings and flanges used in atomic power plants and missile launch pads; the nation's largest producer of horse saddlery and harnesses; Paramount Pictures, a producer, financier, and distributor of motion pictures; Desilu Productions, a producer and distributor of television programs; a horse racing track; the South Puerto Rico Sugar Company; Consolidated Cigar Company, maker of Dutch Master, El Producto, and Muriel cigars; a manufacturer of firefighting equipment; an artillery shell and air-conditioning concern; Brown Paper, a producer of tissue and writing paper with extensive timber holdings; and two large financial institutions, Providence Washington Insurance and the Associates. (The firm also tried to acquire Armour Meat, Allis-Chalmers, and Sinclair Oil, but failed.)

In all, Gulf & Western controlled nearly 70 firms by 1968. Its corporate purchases accounted for 84 percent of the firm's rise to the heights of the *Fortune* 500. But there was a price to be paid. By the early 1980s Gulf & Western had become what *Fortune* characterized as "a conceptually messy agglutination"; ultimately it had to implement a massive billion-dollar divestiture plan to sell off its operations in zinc, movie theaters, cigars, mattresses and furniture, video games, and Madison Square Garden. It began retracing its steps. The "urge to purge" had replaced the "urge to merge"; and Martin S. Davis (who succeeded the great conglomerator Charles G. Bluhdorn as Gulf & Western's chief executive) ruefully confided to *Business Week*: "Bigness is not a sign of strength. In fact, the opposite is true."[7]

In 1960, ITT was a manufacturer of telecommunications equipment and an operator of international telephone systems. It ranked 51st on *Fortune*'s 500 list. Dissatisfied with its status as "primarily a one-product company," Harold S. Geneen had ITT embark on a systematic diversification program which, between 1961 and 1969, netted 74 domestic and 66 foreign acquisitions valued at roughly $4 billion. ITT became involved in the production of seemingly endless lines of dissimilar goods and services: telephone handsets, battlefield radar, bathroom and kitchen fixtures, automotive brakes, lumber and timber, grass and plant seed (O. M. Scott, Burpee), Wonder bread and Hostess Twinkies (Continental Baking), Sheraton Hotels, insurance (Hartford), home building (Levitt), car rentals (Avis), fire-extinguishing equipment (Grinnell), books (Bobbs-Merrill), and business and technical training schools. It maintained Washington's "hot lines" to Moscow, staffed the Air Force Distant Early Warning (DEW) System and the giant Ballistic Missile Early Warning System (BMEWS) in Greenland and Alaska, and produced navigation equipment for the NAVSTAR satellites.

By the 1970s, ITT had grown into a corporation whose subsidiaries (according to its annual report) were "constantly at work around the clock—in 67 nations on six continents" in activities extending "from the Arctic to the Antarctic and quite literally from the bottom of the sea to the moon." The game plan and the tactics used to carry out this growth led Paul Costman Cabot, dean of the Boston financial community, long-time director of J. P. Morgan & Co., and one-time treasurer of Harvard, to reflect: "It seems that each generation is cursed with problems all born of greed and the lust for power."[8] But here again, as with G&W, the financial wizardry undergirding spectacular growth exacted a price. By the 1980s, Geneen's house of cards began to crumble. The company had become what *Fortune* labeled "a museum of the investment and management ideas of the Sixties," and Geneen's successors were forced to launch a vast divestiture program involving more than 40 subsidiaries—a program described by one Wall Street analyst as "the biggest sell-off of assets in corporate history."

The Allegis affair provides yet another parable for a business era of merger, consolidation, and restructuring. The moral is that there is no salvation through acquisition—that the dream of assembling a corporate empire by shuffling and leveraging assets is an empty one. Not so long ago, in 1979, United Airlines was already a colossus. By any measure, it was the largest investor-owned airline in the world. In addition, it owned and operated the Westin Hotel chain, which managed 61 hotels here and overseas. It owned such real estate landmarks as New York's Plaza Hotel.

In 1979, Richard Ferris, who had risen through the ranks of United's hotel and food service system, became chief executive. His grand design was to convert United Airlines into a one-stop, full-service travel center. He was prepared to forsake short-term profits to pursue his vision of market dominance and big returns. Ferris proceeded to build a travel conglomerate. In June 1985, he bought Hertz for $587 million. Four months later, he paid $750 million for the Pacific routes of Pan American World Airways. In 1986, he bought the Hilton International Company for $980 million. Finally, the emerging empire was given a new name; after a year's deliberation and the expenditure of more than $7 million, United Airlines became the Allegis Corporation.

But alas, there was unrest in the empire and grumbling on Wall

Street. Passengers complained about service. Hotel and airline bookings became confused as the reservations system, an important competitive weapon for United, began to deteriorate. Most threatening, both the airline's pilots and the Coniston Partners offered to buy Allegis and dismantle it. Their contention was that the breakup value of the parts was greater than the corporation as a whole—synergism in reverse. In his scramble to fend off a takeover by the Coniston Partners as well as the pilots, Ferris proposed to take on $3 billion in new debt to finance a $60-a-share payout to stockholders. It was a debt burden that flabbergasted stockholders and Wall Street.

The denouement came suddenly—at midnight on June 9, 1987, when the Allegis board unceremoniously relieved Ferris of his command and replaced him with Frank A. Olson. Olson promptly announced his intention to de-merge the travel conglomerate by selling off the Westin and Hilton International chains for an estimated $2.2 billion, and Hertz for an estimated $850 million. Finally, Olson proposed to scrap the six-week-old Allegis logo and to ask the shareholders to approve a new name—United Airlines. The corporation had come full circle.

Allegis was one more poignant reminder that much of the money lavished on the huge corporate consolidation movement of the last two decades may well have been squandered.

The current divestiture and deconglomeration wave does not mean that the empire-building that preceded it was a socially harmless and socially costless experiment. The fact that merger-happy managements are now being punished for their earlier mistakes—that the market is now making them pay the price for poor judgment—does not mean that society has escaped unscathed. For society, as for individuals, there is no such thing as a free lunch. Every action taken in its name exacts an *opportunity cost*—that is, the cost of not having done something else. Two decades of managerial energy devoted to the conglomerate quick-growth game are two decades during which management's attention has been diverted from investment in new plants, new products, and improved manufacturing techniques. The roughly one *trillion* dollars spent since 1980 on exchanging paper claims through takeovers, buyouts, and acquisitions represents an equivalent amount *not* spent on productivity-enhancing equipment or on research and development. The millions of dollars absorbed by legal fees and bankers' commissions are resources *not* plowed back into productive ventures. The funds borrowed by the conglomerateurs are funds *not* available to other firms, especially small businesses. Most significant, perhaps, the enormous physical, intellectual, and psychological investment that management devoted to finding companies to acquire or to fending off takeovers, organizing raids, or designing poison pills could have been used in more productive pursuits. All these are opportunity costs. They are social costs not paid by the merger-spawned giants; they are a burden to us and to the nation's economy. Even if the acquisitive giants are eventually punished for bad planning, society still will pay a price for their mistakes. And that can hardly be construed as a boon to the nation's productivity, technological progress, or international competitiveness.[9]

The debilitating effects of mergers and acquisitions, buyouts and takeovers, whether "friendly" or "hostile," are most sinister with respect to R&D and (real) capital investment—that is, with respect to the nation's industrial future. Following its leveraged buyout, for example, "some 480 of Owens-Corning's 970 research employees have been let go; the research center's budget has been slashed in half (to $45 million); 46 percent of the firm's total work force has been axed or lost in divestitures; and 14 percent of the company's productive capacity has been mothballed. All to generate enough increased cash flow to service $2 billion in debt incurred by the firm as part of a frantic recapitalization plan designed to thwart" a takeover bid.[10] The "recapitalized" Owens-Corning retreated to its cyclically mature markets in autos and housing, while reducing further investment in developing new products and processes.

Other companies have slashed their research and development

commitment in the wake of takeovers. General Electric, shortly after its acquisition of RCA, promptly sold the latter's magnificent $100 million David Sarnoff research center. (Remember the company's discarded motto? "At General Electric progress is our most important product.") Uniroyal, Inc., soon after its leveraged buyout in September 1985, cut back long-term corporate research and development as it spun off divisions. Similarly, Goodyear Tire & Rubber chopped its research and development program by 7 percent in the wake of a restructuring move to fend off Anglo-French raider James Goldsmith.[11]

There is little doubt that spending on research and development in the United States is slowing down at a time when intensified foreign competition suggests the need for accelerating this type of investment. In a recent study, the Battelle Memorial Institute reported that company R&D spending in 1989 would rise by only 4.5 percent. Such spending, Battelle indicates, is being held down by corporate restructurings and buyouts that force managements to concentrate on cash flow to pay interest on the heavy borrowing that invariably accompanies these deals.[12] A National Science Foundation study of 24 companies, while conceding that it is too early to assess the long-run effects, reported that 16 companies which had undergone mergers and acquisitions showed a 4.7 percent drop in R&D spending in 1986 and 1987, while 8 companies that had undertaken LBOs or other restructurings showed an even steeper 12 percent drop.[13] The findings are hardly surprising. Says Margaret Blair, a senior research analyst at the Brookings Institution: "It's hard for me to imagine a scenario where LBOs don't hurt R&D."[14]

While American business continually bemoans its "lost competitiveness," U.S. firms "apparently intend to continue to neglect R&D activity," reports the latest DRI/McGraw-Hill survey of corporate R&D spending plans. The disquieting fact is that, after rising at a hefty 12.7 percent annual clip from 1976 through 1985, R&D outlays have been crawling forward at less than a 6 percent rate. "In real terms," comments Gene Koretz of *Business Week*, "the slowdown has been even more dramatic, with spending growth falling from

TABLE 12

CORPORATE EXPENDITURES ON MERGERS, R&D, AND NET NEW INVESTMENT ($ BILLIONS)

Year	Mergers and Acquisitions	Industry-financed R&D	Net New Nonresidential Investment
1980	$ 33.0	$ 30.9	$ 88.9
1981	67.3	35.9	98.6
1982	60.4	40.1	65.5
1983	52.6	43.5	45.8
1984	126.0	49.1	91.1
1985	145.4	52.6	101.5
1986	204.4	55.7	81.0

Sources: *Mergers & Acquisitions*, May–June 1988; *Statistical Abstract of the United States, 1988*; *Economic Report of the President, 1988.*

a 6.6 percent average rate to 1.8 percent (counting this year). In fact, 1989 will mark the third time in four years that R&D investment has expanded more slowly than the economy itself."[15]

Table 12 dramatically summarizes the opportunity cost of the paper entrepreneurialism generated by merger-mania. Note, for example, that in 1986 American industry spent $204 billion on mergers and acquisitions—more than the $55 billion on R&D and the $81 billion on new plant and equipment combined.

A casino society may provide lucrative employment to the operators of the gaming tables and transient thrills to their clients. But it is unproductive and uncreative. A casino society is a poor framework for promoting the reindustrialization of America or the restoration of its international competitiveness. In the final analysis, a casino society is based on the California Principle: Anything not worth doing at all is worth carrying to wild excess.

11

THE SANTAYANA CURSE

Those who do not learn from history are condemned to repeat it.
—Attributed to George Santayana

What experience and history teach us is this—that people and governments never have learned anything from history, or acted on principles deduced from it.
—Hegel, *Philosophy of History*

A specter is haunting Europe—the prospect that in 1992 all national boundaries are to be obliterated. In 1992 Western Europe is to become a genuinely common market. And how are the captains of industry preparing for the great event? "Merger mania is sweeping Europe," *Fortune* reports. "No combination seems too far out, and even hostile takeovers are in."[1] Individual deals are bigger than ever: In 1988 alone, Sweden's electrical engineering giant ASEA merged with its Swiss counterpart, Brown Boveri; France's Cie. Financière de Suez acquired Société Générale, an industrial conglomerate that ranks as Belgium's biggest company; and after a bitter takeover battle, Nestlé swallowed the British candymaker Rountree. In every country, politicians are trying to create "national champions" by merging large companies into a single dominant monster. Predicts the manager of a London-based investment fund: "Over the next decade Europe is going to experience the kind of intensification of M&A activity that the U.S. went through in the 1980s."[2] Mergers and consolidations are indispensable, the Europeans say, if the "old continent" is to combat the brooding omnipresence of American and Japanese giants in world markets.

At the same time, American policy-makers justify their own pro-merger, pro-concentration policy with the identical argument—and point the accusing finger in the opposite direction. Facilitating U.S. mergers and acquisitions, promoting corporate bigness, and emasculating the antimerger law, they say, are the kinds of bold new departures needed to enable American firms to challenge foreign rivals and to regain global competitiveness. Late Commerce Secretary Malcolm Baldrige argued incessantly that while U.S. firms had been restrained from consolidating, their foreign competitors had outmerged, outrun, and outdominated them: "For example, in 1960 twenty-seven of the thirty largest industrial companies in the world were United States firms—over ninety percent. In 1984, only ten of those top thirty world-wide industrial companies were United States companies—just one-third. That is a drop of nearly sixty percent."[3] The United States, he and other Reaganauts said, must throw itself into the bigness race. It must "not be stopped by those who are preoccupied with outdated notions about firm size."[4] Some top U.S. business executives agree. They too boldly affirm the "new learning" that "combinations strengthen U.S. companies and help them withstand pressure from foreign competitors." If "our industries are going to survive," they warn, "there have to be additional consolidations to achieve needed economies of scale." Corporate consolidation and bigness, they conclude, are "perhaps the only answer to saving a maximum number of jobs for this country."[5]

Neither the Europeans nor the Americans, however, seem to be aware of their past experience in playing the merger game. On both sides of the Atlantic, industrial statesmen seem oblivious to the uncomfortable parallels between past and present. A look backward is therefore instructive.

Beginning in the 1950s and reaching historic peaks in the 1960s, Europe embarked on a period of unprecedented consolidation. "A fascination with giantism, a mania for mergers, call it what you will," *Fortune* reported in 1970, "but Europe's leading businessmen are infected with it. They are merging companies with such haste and sweep that no label seems quite adequate."[6]

The rationale for the movement was articulated in Jean Jacques Servan-Schreiber's best-seller, *Le Defi Americain* (The American Challenge). The largest corporations, he wrote, "are the ones most likely to undertake the investment and research activities essential to successful competition." Large size "permits the development of an advanced scientific potential" and "pushes the firm into new areas and thereby places it in a position of leadership." If Europe deprived itself of the "dynamism, organization, innovation, and boldness that characterize the giant American corporations," he warned, it would "fall even further behind in the global competitive race." The challenge for European governments, he concluded, was clear: "Creation of large industrial units which are able both in size and management to compete with the American giants," and "choosing 50 to 100 firms which, once they are large enough, would be the most likely to become world leaders of modern technology in their fields." Like some American policy-makers today, he derided European policies that posed obstacles to the corporate mergers and consolidations necessary for attaining international dominance. He too argued that there was no place for an anti-merger policy in what he conceived to be the "new age."[7]

Enthralled with the bigness mystique, Great Britain created the Industrial Reorganization Corporation (IRC), a government body charged with encouraging mergers. The enabling legislation in 1966 cited the "need for more concentration and rationalisation to promote the greater efficiency and international competitiveness of British industry." It contended that many "production units in this country are small by comparison with the most successful companies in international trade, whose operations are often based on a much larger market." It expressed the belief that "the typical company in Britain is too small to achieve long production runs; to take advantage of economies of scale; to undertake effective research and development; to support specialist departments for design and marketing; to install the most modern equipment or to attract the best qualified management." What was needed, it reasoned, was an industrial structure "which will enable us to make the most effective use, in the years ahead, of our resources of skill, management and capital." Mergers, consolidation, and corporate bigness, it concluded, would "secure a lasting improvement in the structure and competitive strength of British industry."

Two years later, in 1968, Prime Minister Harold Wilson called for a restructuring of British industries "on a scale and at a speed such as we have not seen in this century," including a rethinking of Britain's traditional hostility to monopolies and mergers. Accordingly, through a succession of mergers, acquisitions, and consolidations, British automobile production was concentrated into the hands of two firms, British Motor Holdings (including Austin, Morris, and Jaguar), and Leyland Motors (including Rover and Triumph). In 1968, when these two companies fell victim to financial difficulties, the government promoted a merger between them to create British Leyland. The consolidation—creating a monopoly of production in the UK market, and the 5th largest automotive manufacturer in the world at the time—was justified as essential if Britain was to remain in international automobile production.

British Leyland's performance, however, was less than auspicious: Production plunged from more than 900,000 cars in 1972 to 410,000 in 1986; its share of the UK new-car market has dropped from 40 percent in 1968 to less than 18 percent; and since 1979, the firm has accumulated losses totaling $2.29 billion. As a result, the British auto industry became a corporate mendicant, almost totally dependent on government for financial sustenance. According to one account, government support for BL has totaled $5.4 billion over the years since 1975—support which, because of the firm's importance to the British economy, has transcended philosophical differences between Labourites and Conservatives.

The London *Economist* wrote a fitting epitaph to the BL experiment: "Merger after merger . . . was supposed to create a creature strong enough to stop the rot, to realise economies of scale and face up to foreign competition. Then another one was needed." But the strategy failed. The history of British Leyland "is a parable of how such lumping together of good with bad is no match for winnowing out the bad and running the good competitively. Its successive mergers and reorganisations produced a ragbag range of cars that never settled down to win market share from the car companies of America, Japan, France, West Germany and Italy."[8]

The success of Jaguar is an instructive counterpoint to the British Leyland fiasco. Once it was spun off from BL and taken private in 1984, Jaguar became a profitable company. This lends credence to the resolution of British Leyland's problems suggested by the *Economist* as early as 1977: The firm's problems are too large for its management to handle, the magazine's editors observed. Their solution? "Split BL back into its component parts."[9]

In France, the faith in merger-induced bigness was formally codified in the Fifth Plan, adopted in 1966 as a statement of national economic policy: "The Fifth Plan therefore proposes to constitute or, where they already exist, to strengthen a small number of international scale firms or groups capable of standing up to the foreign groups in the main spheres of competition. . . . In most major sectors of industry . . . *the number of such groups should be very limited, often restricted to one or two.*" Bigness and concentration of industry in the hands of one or two "national champions" were to be the keys to meeting *le defi americain*. These, in turn, would require a deliberate government program encouraging consolidation. As articulated at the time by Louis Vallon, a prominent member of the French National Assembly, "French industry cannot compete with American giants without embarking on a major program of mergers."

Steel was one sector in which this policy was implemented. It was designed to allay persistent complaints by French steel executives about the disparity in size between the "small" French firms and the American steel "giants." America, one executive explained, has "U.S. Steel and Bethlehem that are big enough and rich enough to make their power felt anywhere, at any time. . . . [T]here is no counterpart to these giants in the Common Market or more broadly in West Europe."

Eventually, the grounds for this complaint were removed. Beginning in the late 1950s and continuing for two decades, a succession of mergers and acquisitions concentrated the French steel industry into three dominant groups: Usinor and Sacilor in carbon steel and Creusot-Loire in stainless and specialty steel. Contrary to expectations, however, this chain of consolidations did not lead to better economic performance. During the 1970s, productivity in the industry remained lower than for any of France's major competitors. Contrary to forecasts, production levels fell from 1974 onward. France's steel giants devoted their investment to capacity expansion rather than to improving productivity; they became ill-fitted mixtures of old and new plants, with higher operating costs.

By September 1978, France's largest steel producers had accumulated losses amounting to approximately $8 billion. In that year, confronted with the industry's warning that "emergency measures were the only alternative to bankruptcy on a massive scale," the government was impelled to bail out the industry (and, in effect, to nationalize it) by converting a portion of the industry's losses into state equity holdings, and by covering the remainder with state loans and guarantees. A new holding company was created, and the state assumed over FF12 billion of debt and added a new FF8 billion loan. (President Mitterand labeled the subsidies and low-interest loan granted to the industry by his conservative predecessors as "13 milliards pour rien"—13 billion for nothing.)

In Italy, the most conspicuous firm on the industrial landscape, and by far the biggest, is the Instituto per la Ricostruzione Industriale (IRI). This state-owned enterprise was created by Mussolini in 1933 to absorb the assets of failing firms and banks during the

Great Depression, as well as to act as a driving force for Italian industrialization. Through five decades of acquisitions and absorptions, IRI has grown to mammoth proportions. It encompasses over 1,000 individual firms, 500,000 workers, and accounts for 5 percent of total national investment, 11 percent of national R&D expenditures, and 3.3 percent of the total national work force (including 6 percent of all manufacturing employment). IRI's operations, reaching from cast iron to ice cream, include: Finsider (the 2nd largest steel producer in Europe, and the 4th largest in the world, controlling nearly 60 percent of the Italian steel industry through more than 40 major iron and steel companies); Alfa Romeo; Alitalia; Stet (telecommunications and electronics); Finmare (90 percent of Italian shipbuilding); and SME (food processing). In addition, IRI controls over 60 banking organizations, representing 17 percent of national banking. Overall, IRI ranks as the third largest industrial corporation outside the United States.

But mergers, acquisitions, consolidations, and corporate bigness have scarcely been conducive to world-class economic performance in Italian industry. On a consolidated basis, IRI posted losses *in every year* from 1973 to 1985; its accumulated debts reached $21 billion by the end of 1978; and by 1980 its losses amounted to $5 million *per day*. Commenting on the firm's performance, the *Economist* pointed out: "It is no good saying that [IRI's losses] look so bad because it is lumbered with all the heavy, basic industries that are in trouble throughout the industrialised world: it was supposed to be an efficient mechanism for adjusting such sectors to adverse structural changes."[10] The Italian government conceded as much in a 1981 document prepared by the Ministry of State Share-Holdings: "The crisis of the largest Italian firm shows its deepest intensity in the public-owned firms: in the last five years they lost more than 9,500 billion lire with an alarming progression that does not give any signal of decreasing. . . . The system of public Shareholdings . . . has become terribly costly in terms of collective resources absorbed, while the results are worsening every day."

It is significant that IRI's current president, Romano Prodi, one of Italy's leading economists, is attempting to return the giant firm to profitability in important part by reducing IRI's size, and by divesting a number of operating divisions (including Alfa Romeo). Prodi's credo is "Tagliare, tagliare, e ancora tagliare" (Cut, cut, and cut again).

Japan provides a fitting counterpoint to the European experience. In motor vehicles, for example, the Ministry of International Trade and Industry (MITI) sought as early as 1953 to concentrate production of automobiles in one or at most two established firms (Nissan, Toyota), and to preclude new entry. When three new firms (Mitsubishi, Fuji, Mazda) commenced automobile production, cutting the combined Toyota-Nissan market share from three-quarters to less than one-half, MITI was alarmed. Government authorities worried "that a large number of competing auto firms could only result in disaster. The ministry also reasoned that excessive competition among the manufacturers would be detrimental to bringing the Japanese auto industry into a competitive position with the American 'Big Three.' " Prime Minister Ikeda voiced his concern that "the Japanese automobile manufacturers will not become competitive with General Motors and Ford under the current [competitive, unregulated entry] condition." Yet another government official warned that "in the light of world trends in the industries, and in the light of the present situation in our country . . . six [auto] companies are too many [and] five or six will not be possible."

In 1961 MITI announced plans to consolidate Japanese automakers into just three large concerns, to limit each of these firms to a single segment of the market, and to bar newcomers (including Honda) from the field. In the face of intense industry opposition, however, MITI abandoned its plan. By 1965, Japan had eight highly competitive car companies; by 1984, the number had grown to nine, and Japanese automakers had prevailed against the world—and against their own government's faith in bigness by consolidation. The effect on performance in markets around the world requires no adumbration.

Nor was the automobile industry unique. Instead, the Japanese experience was similar in a variety of other industries, including computers, electronics, steel, and machine tools. So for propagandists of bigness to justify their cause by pointing to megamergers abroad is doubly ironic and depressing. It *was not* done in Japan. It *was* tried in Europe, where it failed miserably. To now shape the U.S. economy according to mythical precepts of what is imagined to have been the experience abroad would be (as Dr. Johnson said of second marriages) a triumph of hope over reality.

U.S. experience reinforces this conclusion. The first major American merger movement began in the late 1800s, and reached its zenith at the turn of the century. Within five years, however, it had collapsed in economic failure and financial panic. Between 1895 and 1904, some 3,000 firms disappeared as a result of mergers, acquisitions, and corporate consolidations. Seventy-five percent of these deals represented simultaneous fusions of at least five firms; 26 percent involved combinations of ten or more firms at a single stroke.[11] Eighty-six very large corporate consolidations (valued at $1 million or more) were consummated between 1887 and 1897, representing a combined capitalized value of $1.4 billion. Mergermania reached its apogee during the next three years, when 149 combinations were undertaken, with a combined capitalized value of $3.8 billion, an enormous sum in that day, and more than double the value of all corporate deals conducted during the entire preceding decade.[12]

The catalyst was the promoter, who captured spectacular profits for making deals. The promoter persuaded participants "to exchange their stock (on very generous terms) for the shares of a new holding company; he distributed the rest of the bonds and shares of the holding company to an eager investing public; and then he so often manipulated these shares on the stock exchanges as to reap fortunes for all those on the inside, including himself."[13]

Promotional profits, not economic performance, drove the game. In fact, the promoter needed no hands-on industrial expertise to ply his craft:

> A man might bring together a group of steel companies in January, a group of woolen companies in August, and a group of match companies in December. What he needed was not specialized knowledge, but persuasive salesmanship, coupled with the ability to command the millions and the investment-sales machinery of a large banking house, and to command also the services of astute corporation lawyers and stock-market operators. Having launched his holding company, pocketed his stock, and arranged to distribute part or all of it through the stock market, the promoter might pass on to fresh woods and pastures new.[14]

Promoter profits were fabulous for that time. (Some are even impressive eighty years later.) In the 1901 consolidation creating the U.S. Steel Corporation, promoter profits totaled an estimated $62.5 million, of which the lion's share went to the Morgan investment bank for implementing the deal. Other deals and promoter profits included the American Tobacco Company ($10.6 million), the glucose trust ($4.5 million), the asphalt trust ($3 million), and the starch trust ($722,677).[15]

The deals generated a blizzard of new issues of all manner of stocks and bonds that, fueled by speculation, traded in ever more inflated terms. And in a laissez-faire age of financial buccaneering, opportunities for manipulation were plentiful. The "fine art of organizing pools to buy and sell securities in huge bulk on the Stock Exchange and thus push stock prices up and down, taking profits along the way from the pockets of unorganized and unlucky speculators" reached a high degree of perfection.[16] With fees and promoter profits so handsome and ripe for the picking, trivialities like operating efficiency, costs, or physical productivity were hardly of pressing concern. If they were taken into account at all, they were (to use Frederick Lewis Allen's phrase) merely "accessories after the fact."

Perhaps predictably, then, the real economic benefits in terms of better operating efficiency, lower production costs, and improved technological innovation were highly dubious. Surveying the record from a vantage point twenty years later, economist Eliot Jones concluded that the deals, combinations, and consolidations had not noticeably improved economic performance. Many of the combines that had been put together in slapdash fashion collapsed outright. Most of those that survived did so for reasons unrelated to the deals themselves or to any real economic efficiencies flowing from them. Instead, their "success" was due more to such advantages as patents already held, monopoly control of raw materials and critical resources, or discriminatory transportation rates (as in the notorious case of the Standard Oil Trust).[17] In fact, by 1903, 37 new industrial "trusts," having a combined capitalized value exceeding $600 million, had "disintegrated" or were defunct; 13 others (capitalized at $500 million) were suffering serious financial difficulties.[18] Another economic analyst, writing in the 1930s, corroborated these economic failures. Examining 156 primary industrial mergers and acquisitions, Livermore calculated that 33 percent of them had failed early on; 6 percent had failed at a later date; and 11 percent were classified into what he labeled the "limping" group. If "successes" attributable to patents or monopoly power were excluded, the effective failure rate rose to nearly 60 percent.[19]

Cochran and Miller found that not only had the anticipated economies of corporate bigness failed to materialize, but a more deeply rooted problem had arisen. As a result of deal-mania, "Men trained only in banking and finance now began to control manufacturing and transportation. Men to whom financial expediency was always the first consideration, now began to control the strategy of long-run planning in production and service." This development, they concluded, shackled the economy with the worst of two worlds—stagnant industrial leadership and reckless financial control. It "gradually dulled the initiative of erstwhile American entrepreneurs and straitened their inventive and organizing genius. . . . Since [their] superiors either were unavailable, or else were opposed to experimenting with new schemes, lest it disturb their financial arrangements, conservatism became as characteristic of many branches of American industry as recklessness had become characteristic of finance."[20]

While the real economic gains were slight, however, the financial fallout was not. Industrial stock prices plunged 65 percent on the New York exchanges in 1903 and catapulted the country into a financial panic—as consolidations tottered or collapsed, as investors balked, as syndicates were unable to move the huge inventories of securities they had contracted to underwrite, and as speculators unloaded shares into a declining market. An economic downturn brought deal-mania to an end by imparting a final, devastating blow to the shaky financial structures that had been thrown together in such furious haste.[21]

Deal-mania remained in remission until the 1920s when, once again, it gripped the body economic. Corporate mergers and financial speculation—and the proliferation of an especially vulnerable form of corporate organization, the holding company—mutually reinforced each other in driving the economy to the precipice of recklessness, then pushing it over into a seemingly bottomless chasm. It was an era not unlike our own when, as John Kenneth Galbraith points out, corporations found it more profitable to engage in the production of financial speculation rather than the production of goods.[22] Banks became increasingly eager to add financial fuel to the flames. And the stock exchange once again became a great gambling casino—less a register of fundamental economic prospects, and more an instrument for what Galbraith called "manipulative artifice."

Corporate deal-making proceeded at an escalating, breakneck pace. It was (Allen wrote in 1935) "a positive mania for mergers," and "a dull week that brought no marriage announcements in the financial pages."[23] In all, an estimated 12,000 firms disappeared through merger, acquisition, or consolidation between 1919 and 1930. One fertile ground for deal-making involved electric and gas utility consolidations. Another comprised combinations between second- and third-tier firms in an industry to create tightly knit oligopolies in such fields as steel, food products, chemicals, and metals. (National Dairy alone engaged in 331 acquisitions in the decade ending in 1933.) A third fertile field involved mergers for diversification and conglomeration.[24]

A major preoccupation of the deal-makers during this era was *pyramiding*—organizing holding companies to control holding companies that controlled other holding companies. This they found to be an excellent device for maximizing their span of control while minimizing the investment needed to realize these imperialistic designs. By investing enough in one corporation to control it, by next creating a holding company to float stocks and bonds to the public, by using these proceeds to acquire a controlling position in another firm, and by repeating the process all over again, a small initial investment could be parlayed into a vast economic domain—all premised, of course, on an eager investing public and constantly expanding cash flows.

The architecture involved can best be appreciated by considering one small part of the vast pyramid of holding companies constructed by utility magnate Samuel Insull: The Tidewater Power Company in North Carolina "was controlled by the Seaboard Service Company, and the Seaboard by the National Public Service Corporation, and the National by the National Electric Power Company, and this National Electric Power Company by Middle West Utilities, and Middle West was controlled jointly by Corporate Securities Company of Chicago and Insull Utility Investments, Inc.—which in turn were controlled by the Insull family and by the banking house of Halsey, Stuart & Co." In this fashion, Insull came to control "several hundred electric light and power plants and gas plants and other properties scattered from Maine to Texas and Oklahoma."[25]

Insull was not unique. Goldman Sachs created the Goldman Sachs Trading Corp., which created the Shenandoah Corporation, which created the Blue Ridge Corporation, at each step selling bonds to buy stock in the next step. In Europe Ivar Kreuger created a similar edifice of enormous debt, some of it in bonds that he had forged and issued against the assets of unwitting creditors. All used the miracle of leverage and the convenience of the holding company to link more and more industrial, financial, and transportation operations together under increasingly intricate (and vulnerable) layers of financial management.

For its promoters, the holding company seemed to offer an endless chain of profits from consolidation, speculation, and stock market manipulation. Because (with appropriate accounting legerdemain) holding companies could be made "to show big profits it was easy to raise money to finance them. . . . Because it was so easy to show profits, the stock could be watered and the magnates at the center of things could make much money through financing operations. Because so much money could be made, the systems became more and more ambitious and tried to get hold of more and more operating companies." So attractive was this device that Insull eventually conglomerated his utility empire by acquiring paper production facilities, textile mills, a tire-fabric company, shoe manufacturing, and real estate development properties.[26]

Banks gleefully joined in the game. "They it was who, with the sleepless aid of their corporation lawyers, put into effect many if not most of the devices by which the promoters and organizers of corporations might do as they pleased. . . . During these years an endless stream of new issues of securities poured forth from their offices and were swallowed up by an eager investing public."[27]

Throughout, the game was tainted with the unmistakable strain of speculative manipulation. Stock trading "pools" provided an easy way to fleece a gullible investing public. A pool manager would take a position in a particular stock:

> This buying would increase prices and attract the interest of people watching the [stock market] tape across the country. The interest of the latter would then be further stimulated by active selling and buying, all of which gave the impression that something big was afloat. Tipsheets and market commentators would tell of exciting developments in the offing. If all went well, the public would come in to buy, and prices would rise on their own. The pool manager would then sell out, pay himself a percentage of the profits, and divide the rest with his investors.[28]

Mergers, acquisitions, and the formation of holding companies multiplied the opportunities for insiders to pluck easy profits from the public; they bought early, sold early, and conveniently "avoided the rush."

As one result of this frenzied finance, corporate debt exploded. In the public utility field, debt grew by 181 percent over the decade of the 1920s. For industrial companies generally, it expanded by 172 percent. And for financial concerns, it grew by 389 percent. All told, debt in the economy proliferated at a rate triple that of the growth of national wealth and income during the decade.[29]

Nor was the game lacking for apologists, who sought to cloak it in the mantle of economic legitimacy. Then, as now, it was avowed that the corporate structures produced by these deals "made for speed, for efficiency, for harmony; they did away with red tape; and they put the affairs of the corporation in question in what the insiders naturally considered to be the most capable and deserving hands—to wit, their own hands and those of their friends."[30] Ohio State economics professor Charles Amos Dice was effusive at the time, praising the deal-makers for what he called "their vision for the future," and their freedom from "the heavy armor of tradition."[31] Then, as now, Wall Street experts solemnly warned against any government interference because, they insisted, to intervene would "deny investors the means of recognizing economies which are now proved, skill which is now learned, and inventions which are almost unbelievable."[32]

Of course, these rationalizations were of no avail when the accumulated financial excesses, reckless deals, ramshackle corporate structures, and stratospheric stock price spirals crashed in 1929, ushering in the economic devastation of the 1930s. In the aftermath, Samuel Insull went to Greece, Kreuger to a Paris store to buy a pistol to shoot himself, and Goldman Sachs, "its breathtaking innovations all but worthless, retreated to a greatly chastened conservatism."[33]

While the Great Depression was the product of a variety of forces, it is indisputable that the deal-mania of the twenties was central among them. A financial meltdown—wrought by the arithmetic of reverse leverage—relentlessly ground out its inexorable results. As John Kenneth Galbraith clinically describes it, the

> . . . interruption of the dividends [in holding companies] meant default on the bonds, bankruptcy, and the collapse of the structure. Under these circumstances, the temptation to curtail investment in operating plant in order to continue dividends was obviously strong. The latter, in turn, curtailed earnings and helped bring down the corporate pyramids. When this happened, even more retrenchment was inevitable. Income was earmarked for debt repayment. Borrowing for new investment became impossible.

Contrived upon nothing more than the shifting sands of speculative expectations, the elaborate financial edifice now collapsed. As Galbraith concludes: "A corporate system better designed to continue and accentuate a deflationary spiral" would be hard to imagine.[34]

Once again, then, corporate mergers, acquisitions, and deals had failed to promote real economic performance. Once again, mergers and acquisitions had become vehicles for a bigger, broader speculative game—a game of financial delusion and deception. And once again, they brought economic collapse in their wake, both for those who profited from them, as well as for a nation whose economic fortunes became a pawn in an economically destructive, sterile game.

On guard in front of the U.S. Archives in Washington is the marble statue of a majestic lion. Its pedestal bears the inscription (and warning): "What is past is prologue." It attracts little attention.

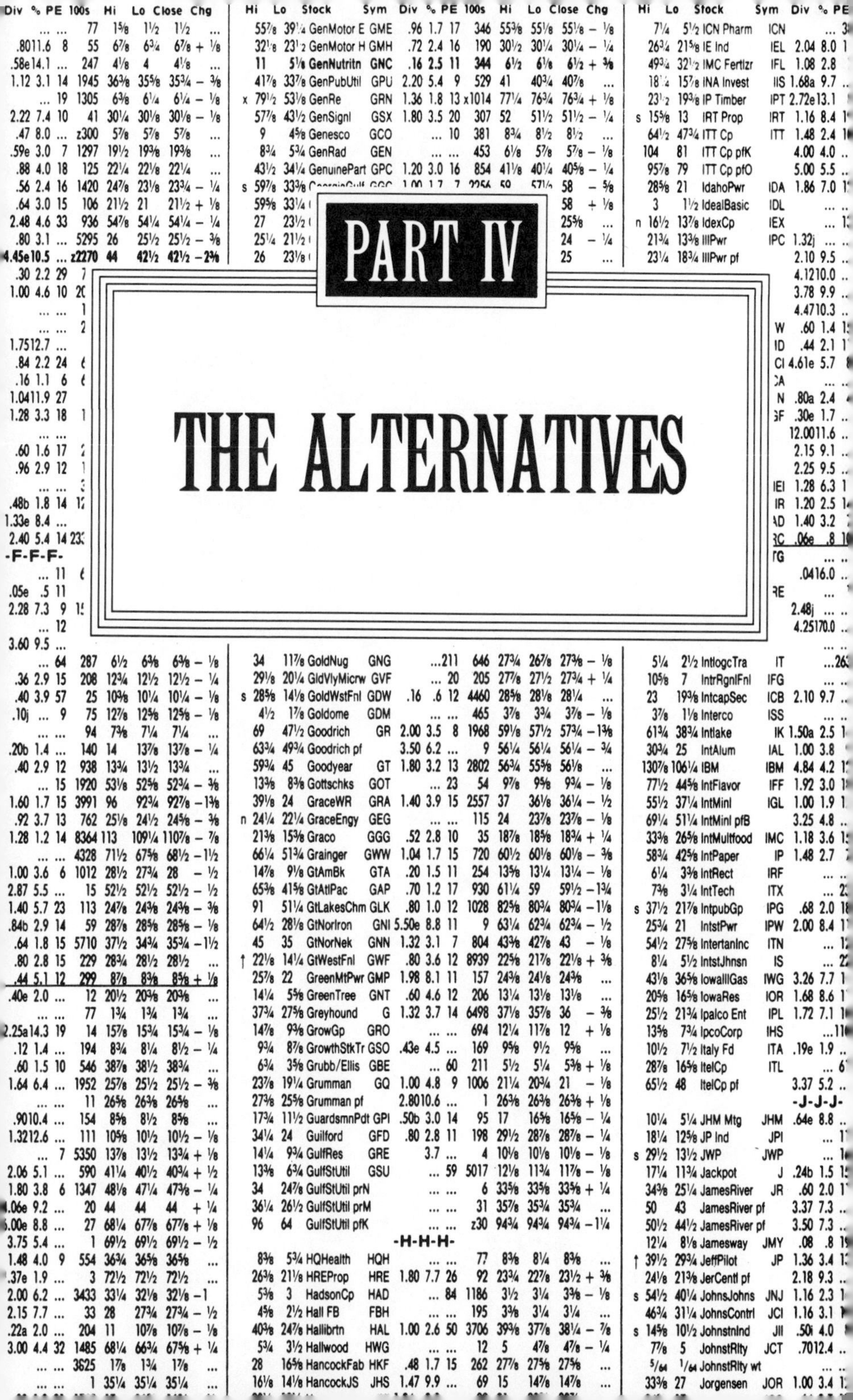

PART IV

THE ALTERNATIVES

12

COWBOY CAPITALISM

That's life in America. 'Tis a gloryous big fight, a rough an' tumble fight, a Donnybrook fair three thousan' miles wide an' a ruction on ivry block. Head an' han's an' feet an' th' pitchers on th' wall. No holds barred. Fight fair but don't f'rget th' other lad may not know where th' belt line is. No polisman in sight. A man's down with twinty on top iv him wan minyit. Th' next he's settin' on th' pile usin' a base-ball bat on th' neighbor next below him. "Come on, boys, f'r 'tis growin' late, an' no wan's been kilt yet. Glory be, but this is th' life!"

—Mr. Dooley

The Dodge City barroom brawl is staple fare in the grade-C oater. The scene is familiar: Writhing, wrestling combatants, smashing one another with chairs, whiskey bottles, and timber, crashing through tables and doors and windows, swinging from chandeliers. It's a no-holds-barred, hell-bent-for-leather melee of flying bodies, shattering glass, leg bites, and roundhouse rights, amid a roar of yowls and howls and screams. It is pure, unalloyed exuberance, totally lacking in rules or etiquette.

The scene captures the kind of public policy advocated by devotees of cowboy capitalism. What is the best government policy toward business and industry? *No* government policy. What is the best public policy toward corporate mergers and acquisitions? *No* public policy. What is the ideal stance toward raids, takeovers, and deal-mania generally? *No* public stance! Concerned about exploding debt loads? The leveraging of corporate America? Ramshackle financial gimmickry? Speculative madness? Anticompetitive consolidations? Increased concentration of corporate control? No need to worry. "Free" markets—defined as the absence of government interference—will solve society's economic problems. It is Dodge City *déjà vu*—with one difference: The honest, incorruptible sheriff, tall in the saddle, is conspicuous by his absence.

Free markets, the cowboy capitalists tell us, will correct all abuses. Free markets will allay all concerns. How do we know? Because "natural" economic forces are constantly working according to the dictates of inexorable "natural" laws—the functioning and ends of which these analysts have comprehended in their entirety.

As Robert Bork articulates it, "the environment to which the business firm must adapt is defined, ultimately, by social wants and the social costs of meeting them. The firm that adapts to the environment better than its rivals tends to expand. The less successful firm tends to contract—perhaps, eventually, to become extinct."[1] Corporate deal-mania is an essential element in this process of economic evolution and natural selection. It is an indispensable instrument in the vital process of "restructuring." Admittedly, the process is painful. But, the cowboy capitalists insist, it is essential.

As described by Michael C. Jensen,

> Restructurings are frequently wrenching events in the lives of those linked to the involved organizations—the managers, employees, suppliers, customers and residents of surrounding communities. Restructurings usually involve transfers of ownership, and major organizational changes (such as shifts in corporate strategy) to meet new competition or market conditions, increased use of debt, and a flurry of recontracting with managers, employees, suppliers and customers. This activity sometimes results

> in expansion of resources devoted to certain areas and at other times in contractions involving plant closings, layoffs of top-level and middle managers, staff and production workers, and reduced compensation. Change due to corporate restructuring requires people and communities associated with the organization to adjust the ways they live, work and do business.

But, Jensen assures us, these bone-jarring changes are indispensable to the economic life process. The market for corporate control "is the arena in which alternative management teams compete for the rights to manage corporate resources." Corporate deal-mania thus "plays an important role in: (1) generating organizational change, (2) motivating the efficient utilization of resources, and (3) protecting shareholders when the corporation's internal controls and board-level controls are slow, clumsy, or break down entirely." Despite appearances, astronomical debt loads too are beneficial, because they precipitate "the crisis to motivate cuts in expansion programs and the sale of those divisions which are more valuable outside the firm," while forcing "a complete rethinking of the organization's strategy and structure." The process is a "messy and unattractive way" to combat our economic performance problems. But it is the "most effective treatment we have for this disease."[2]

Nor should greater industry concentration and corporate giantism be any cause for alarm. Why? Because when and where they arise, these too are manifestations of "natural" economic forces ineluctably working to achieve beneficial outcomes. Again, Robert Bork reassures us: Where they occur, merger-induced trends toward concentration are "prima facie evidence that greater concentration is socially desirable. The trend indicates that there are emerging efficiencies or economies of scale . . . which make larger size more efficient. This increased efficiency is valuable to the society at large, for it means that fewer of our available resources are being used to accomplish the same amount of production and distribution. By striking at such trends," Bork warns, we deny "the realization of those very efficiencies that competition is supposed to encourage."[3] According to William Baxter, President Reagan's first antitrust chief, government interference with corporate deal-mania "would be an error of very substantial magnitude."[4]

As the cowboy capitalists see it, there are only two serious threats to this "natural" Darwinian process. The first is formal cartel agreements among rivals to fix prices and to lessen (or eliminate) competition between themselves. Second, and the cowboy capitalists claim, far more serious, is the anticompetitive predilection of government itself. Federal Trade Commission chairman Daniel Oliver unequivocally declares that "the principal source of restraints on competition is government—the State." Why? Because government is "lobbied by the politically strong, i.e., the relatively wealthy, who face an uncertain future at the hands of the market. Together the politically strong and the legislators devise legislation to limit competition"—including "the multitude of barriers to international trade that have been erected over the years, and that continue to be erected, by statute and through administrative proceedings" in order to shelter domestic producers from foreign competition.[5] Government, in short, is the prime villain in the piece.

The upshot for public policy is clear: Don't meddle. Don't interfere with the natural order of things. Whatever happens must happen. Whatever is is right. *Tout s'arrangera!* is a programmatic imperative the Reagan administration zealously embraced. For eight years, ardent Reaganauts assiduously emasculated the nation's merger policy. They brazenly defied congressional intent and judicial precedent. They promulgated "guidelines" in 1982, and again in 1984, that gutted merger policy, and that made challenges to even the biggest mergers more difficult and less likely. They tolerated corporate consolidations that violated even their own lax standards. They launched their proposed "Merger Modernization Act" in 1986—a broadside effort to have Congress formally transmogrify the merger law. They slashed antitrust budgets and personnel. And they presided over the most voracious corporate feeding frenzy in industrial history.[6]

As a guidepost for public policy, however, cowboy capitalism is hopelessly flawed. It simply is *not* true, for example, that self-interested profit maximization automatically and always is congruent with the national interest. After all, drug pushers, muggers, and those who sell national security secrets all operate on the principle of private profit maximization. Who would argue that their pursuit of private profits promotes the national welfare? As classical conservatives like Jeremy Bentham well understood, it is not enough to shout "Laissez-faire!" and oppose all government action: "To say that a law is contrary to natural liberty, is simply to say that it is a law: for every law is established at the expense of liberty—the liberty of Peter at the expense of the liberty of Paul."[7] If individual rights were absolute and unlimited, they would mean license to commit the grossest abuses against society.

Gainsaying the role of government as rule-maker and arbiter is simplistic—and disingenuous. As Thomas Hobbes observed three hundred years ago, "During the time men live without a common Power to keep them all in awe, they are in that condition which is called Warre; and such a warre, as is every man, against every man. . . . In such condition, there is no place for Industry; because the fruit thereof is uncertain; and consequently no Culture of the Earth; no Navigation, nor use of the commodities that may be imported by Sea; no commodious Building; no Instruments of moving, and removing such things as require much force; no Knowledge of the face of the Earth; no account of Time; no Arts; no Letters; no Society." It is a "natural" state of affairs—but one in which life is "solitary, poore, nasty, brutish, and short."[8]

Breezy declarations about "natural" economic forces and "the survival of the fittest" ignore the critical question—"fittest" to do what? Admittedly, a life of barroom brawling might well be expected to produce a species fit for this activity. But would this be productive? Would it be economically desirable? Would it contribute to an improved standard of living? Would it enhance the economic performance of the nation? As economist John Bates Clark warned long ago:

> In our worship of the survival of the fit under free natural selection we are sometimes in danger of forgetting that the conditions of the struggle fix the kind of fitness that shall come of it; that survival in the prize ring means fitness for pugilism, not for bricklaying nor philanthropy; that survival in predatory competition is likely to mean something else than fitness for good and efficient production; and that only from strife with the right kind of rules can the right kind of fitness emerge.[9]

The cowboy capitalists delight in decrying anticompetitive government policies which, they say, are the prime evil to be guarded against. But they conveniently ignore the fact that government does not operate in a vacuum, and that anticompetitive government policies are advocated by private economic interests (and their powerful lobbies), which are able to manipulate government and subvert it to serve their own ends. They ignore (or are not cognizant of) the fact that in a representative democracy, disproportionate *economic* size produces disproportionate influence in the *political* arena as well. They ignore the fact that once permitted to attain massive size, corporate giants can mobilize the vast political resources at their command—executives and unions, suppliers and subcontractors, governors and mayors, senators and representatives, Republicans and Democrats—in order to bend public policy to their own devices. They ignore the fundamental principle of political economy, laid down by Richard Ely in 1903, that it is a "necessary outcome of human nature that those persons who are to be controlled should enter politics in order that they may either escape the control, or shape it to their own ends."[10] They fail to recognize the obvious fact—that the giant corporation is inevitably as much a political institution as it is an economic organization.

Thus, corporate complexes can lobby the state to immunize them from foreign competition, and to protect them from the self-inflicted consequences of their own mistakes, but at exorbitant expense to the public (as the steel industry has done since the 1960s). They can capture the regulatory power of the state, pervert it into an instrument of cartelization and monopolization, and luxuriate in a cozy cost-plus environment (as the trucking and airline industries did for decades). They can lobby the state for succor, subsidy, and financial sustenance (as the nuclear power industry does). They can extract tax favors, tax privileges, and tax loopholes (as General Motors recently demonstrated in using its Saturn project to whipsaw states and communities to obtain a bonanza of free land, tax holidays, and low-interest government loans). Once they are permitted to attain giant size, corporate complexes acquire a unique sabotage power—the capacity to threaten to shut down operations, and to inflict economic catastrophe on society—if their demands are not acceded to (as defense contractors have repeatedly demonstrated in forcing government compensation for cost overruns and weapons deficiencies). And if they are big enough and incompetent enough, corporate giants can enjoy the ultimate perversion of free enterprise—government bailouts—because they are perceived to be too big to be allowed to fail. As Chrysler, Lockheed, and Continental Illinois amply affirm, corporate complexes can survive not because they are better, but because they are bigger, not because they are fitter, but because they are fatter.[11]

Because they take no account of the political economy of power, the cowboy capitalists are like Henry David Thoreau's neighbors who, he said, "invite the devil in at every angle and then prate about the garden of Eden and the fall of man."

There is also something ludicrous about a policy that attacks trivial transgressions among the pygmies while permitting corporate elephants to freely roam the Darwinian jungles. It is like a theater of the absurd. Reaganauts boastfully bash price-fixing among kosher food concerns, while giving their blessing to corporate combinations between the world's very largest oil companies. It is a world where dry-snuff purveyors and lawyers representing indigent clients are ruthlessly smashed, while joint ventures linking the American auto oligopoly with its major foreign rivals are permitted to proliferate unmolested. It is an Alice-in-Wonderland world, where inconsequential acquisitions involving condoms and brass rods are struck down as threats to the nation's economic survival, while the largest airlines are permitted to consolidate and erect monopoly fortress hubs across the country. It is *opera buffa*, as Raymond Benton points out, when the public is gravely lectured, "that a small-town grocery store that has 75 percent of the local market is a greater threat to freedom than the transnational mega-enterprise commanding resources and generating revenues exceeding those of most nation states."[12]

The cowboy capitalists ignore the further fact that beyond some threshold, corporate deal-mania feeds, and is fed by, speculative financial gimmickry. Beyond some point, it subverts and reverses priorities, distorting the capital markets into casinos poorly suited to facilitate real economic work. It happened in the massive turn-of-the-century merger-mania. It characterized the speculative deal-mania of the roaring twenties. It occurred during the Go-Go 1960s. And it is the unmistakable trademark of deal-mania in the roaring eighties. Speculation, as John Maynard Keynes observed from the depths of the last Great Depression, "may do no harm as bubbles on a steady stream of enterprise. But the position is serious when enterprise becomes the bubble on a whirlpool of speculation. When the capital development of a country becomes a by-product of the activities of a casino, the job is likely to be ill-done."[13] Financial markets become ends rather than means. Then, real economic activity (production, jobs, investment, research, innovation) becomes a pawn in a speculative—and ultimately sterile—financial game of paper entrepreneurship and stock share shuffling.

Finally, there is the troubling fact that corporate deal-mania simply does not work. It does not create new plants and production facilities. It does not create new research and development, new products or new jobs. It does not promote production efficiency or technological innovation. And it does not enhance international competitiveness. Like the barroom brawl, corporate deal-mania ignites action-packed sound and fury. It makes for an exhilarating spectacle. But in the end, it serves no productive purpose. In the end, like the barroom brawl, it leaves nothing but destruction in its wake.[14]

Just as the lawless Western town becomes a refuge for cattle rustlers and gunslingers, so the lawless economy becomes a haven for corruption and artifice. Fraud, force, and fear predominate. Insider-trading scams and securities swindles proliferate. Conspiracies to rig financial markets spin a vast, interconnected web of traders, marriage brokers, managements, and arbitrageurs. Dennis Levine in mergers and acquisitions leads to Ivan Boesky in stock arbitrage. Boesky leads to Drexel Burnham in corporate deal-making. And Drexel Burnham leads to Michael Milken, the king of junk bonds. Investment bankers, who arrange corporate mergers and acquisitions, pass tips to traders about impending deals not yet disclosed to the public and receive millions in the profits fleeced from others. Wheelers and dealers camouflage their stock control by "parking" their securities with others, who then share in the booty. Stock prices are put up, or pushed down, to suit rings of traders and dealers. On their covers, prestigious publications like *Business Week* are—in 1989—forced to ask: "Can Market Corruption Be Stopped?" In the process, deal-mania precipitates an even deeper, even more corrosive effect: The chaos it injects into economic lives (John Dewey observed in the aftermath of the Great Crash of 1929) fosters the attitude that "honest and industrious pursuit of a calling or business will not guarantee any stable level of life." It "lessens respect for work and stirs large numbers to take a chance of some adventitious way of getting the wealth."[15] It thus unleashes a destructive, downward spiraling whirlpool—a self-fulfilling prophecy in which speculation begets speculation, and intrigue begets subterfuge.

Dodge City needs a sheriff to maintain law and order, to break up the brawls, and to restore sanity to its inhabitants. So does Wall Street.

13

COALITION CAPITALISM

Every sin is the result of a collaboration.
—Stephen Crane

"Labor and capital ought to get together," said Mr. Hennessy.

"How cud they get anny closer together thin their prisint clinch?" asked Mr. Dooley. "They're so close together now that those that ar-re between thim ar-re crushed to death."
—Mr. Dooley

Coalition capitalism, grounded in "industrial policy," is the neoliberal Left's riposte to the cowboy capitalism of the Right. Lester C. Thurow, economist and dean of the MIT Sloan School of Management, is a leading proponent of this approach. "Interest in industrial policy," Thurow says, "springs from a simple four-letter word—fear. American industry is being beat up by the international competition, and business and labor are both afraid that American industry is going down for the count." There is "a world market and America's market performance leaves much to be desired. . . . What used to work won't work. For the world has changed. In the aftermath of the destruction of World War II, the United States enjoyed three decades of 'effortless superiority.' We had an enormous economic and technological lead. Our per capita GNP was twice that of the next best country—eight times that of the Japanese. Technologically we led the world in almost everything." But, he emphasizes, "the era of 'effortless superiority' is over and we are now in a *competitive world* economy."

As Thurow sees it, the central challenge for public policy "is not 'the market' versus 'planning,' but how planning can be used to improve one's market performance. . . . Whatever one believes about the virtues of unfettered free enterprise, empirical feedback indicates that 'success' is not occurring automatically." He cites as an example the American machine tool industry, which "has lost about 50 percent of its market to the Japanese in the last five years." What is the American answer, he demands. "There has to be one or we won't have the American industries that we need to provide our citizens with jobs and a rising standard of living."[1]

The only option, coalition capitalists argue, is a consciously constructed national "industrial policy," comprising cooperative planning, negotiation, and bargaining on the part of management, labor, and government. "Industrial policies are to a nation what strategic planning is to a firm," Thurow explains. "They outline the basic strategy the nation intends to follow in maximizing economic growth and meeting foreign competition." Industrial policies

> . . . are both an expression of and a vehicle for bringing about a strategic consensus among government, industry, and labor as to the basic directions in which the economy might be moving. Such a strategic consensus allows each of the individual decision makers to undertake actions that will jointly increase the likelihood that all the economy's economic actors will be successful in reaching their desired collective and individual objectives.
>
> Business might, for example, promise new investment and labor changes in work rules if government were willing to help finance additional research-and-development expenditures in a particular industry. Or government might promise changes in

> the tax code which would make it easier to finance new start-up ventures if labor and business would agree to restrain wage and price increases."[2]

Allied steps would include the creation of a ministry of technology; the implementation of a financial infrastructure of public and private banks able to facilitate resource flows and to aid in restructuring sick industries; and the formation of an industrial restructuring board that would include representatives of management, labor, and government.

The goal is to nurture and to institutionalize a "cooperative bubble-up relationship where government, labor, and industry can work together to create world-class competitive American industries." It would be "an educational process—a sharing of information, a foil for industry, labor, and government—so that each can learn about the problems of the others and how they can mutually interact to solve their joint problems." It would "speed up the workings of the market and remove some of the economic pain and suffering that would occur if the market alone were relied upon."[3]

In what they perceive to be a "new" global age, coalition capitalists dismiss traditional American policy favoring competitively structured domestic industries. They "don't care whether General Motors is the only car manufacturing company. It's still in a competitive fight for its life with the Japanese and the Germans. And it doesn't make sense to hamstring General Motors or anybody else with antitrust laws since they must operate in an international competitive environment, whether or not there are other domestic producers."[4] Instead of concerning ourselves about giant American firms that dominate their markets, they contend, the more important question is "How can we encourage an intelligent combination of the second rank and smaller companies so that we might have a second successful giant?"[5] As they survey the choices, they find it "far better that small American companies be crushed by big American companies than that they be crushed by big foreign companies."[6]

Advocates of coalition capitalism urge the country to adopt "front-door industrial policies where the explicit aim is to generate world-class industries. 'Do nothing' simply isn't a viable answer." We must act, they warn, "Not because we want to; but because we have to." Like football teams, national economies "need organization and planning to win. 'Social organization' is not a four-letter word."[7]

Nevertheless, coalition capitalism and its "industrial policy" plank suffer from at least two fatal defects that render them dubious guideposts for better national economic performance.

The first flaw is that coalition capitalism is infected by the intractable problem of coalescing power among vested interest groups that are inherently predisposed to protect themselves, but at the nation's expense. Coalition capitalism naively assumes that in their logrolling and negotiating, powerful private interest blocs will sensibly agree to act in ways, and toward ends, that will promote good economic performance.

But private power blocs may instead coalesce with one another. They may recognize their larger mutual interest in peaceful coexistence, in preserving the status quo, and in aggrandizing their own power and influence. In so doing, they may collaborate in ways that worsen performance and exacerbate the country's economic ills. Coalition capitalists fail to recognize that market control is irresistibly attractive to powerful business and labor interests. It can provide them with immunity from competition. It can enable them to inflate prices and wages. It can permit them to slumber peacefully in a quiet life of inefficiency and technological stagnation. And government participation may only legitimize and cement the counterproductive schemes cooperatively contrived by these coalescing power groups.

Regrettably, this is not a matter of idle theoretical conjecture. It is, in fact, repeatedly affirmed in our own economic experience.[8] The National Recovery Administration (NRA), set up during the Great Depression, was at the outset intended to be precisely the kind of comprehensive management-labor-government cooperation currently advocated by the coalition capitalists. It was sectoral management-labor planning, replete with "codes of fair competition," with overall supervision and enforcement by government. But the results were radically at odds with what was hoped for. The NRA allowed many business groups to cartelize their industries and to raise prices. It enabled some labor groups to raise wages. But it raised the cost of living for most; it reduced production and consumption; and it only tortured an already tormented national economy. In 1934, at the conclusion of congressional hearings on the NRA, Senator Nye was

> . . . forced to the conclusion that the power of monopoly has been greatly increased during the stay of NRA; that invitation to monopoly in the United States is greater than ever before. In view of what amounts to suspension of the antitrust laws, the small independent producers, the small business man generally, whether buyer from, competitor of, or seller to large monopolized industries, and the great mass of ultimate consumers, are seemingly without protection other than that given by the NRA. And the NRA is not giving this protection. On the contrary, it has strengthened, not weakened, the power of monopoly. Whether this is the decided policy of the administration is unimportant; it is the conclusion to be drawn from its actions.[9]

The NRA failed to rescue the country's economy from depression. Instead, as evaluated by Clair Wilcox, it "provided the country with a demonstration of the character and the consequences of cartelization. It showed that industry, when given the power of 'self-government,' could not be trusted to exercise it in the public interest; that enterprise would be handicapped, progress obstructed, and stagnation assured."[10] It is an episode advocates of coalition capitalism seldom discuss.

The nuclear power debacle provides another, more recent illustration of the problem of coalescing power among vested interests. Here is a field where government and industry have cooperated for decades to promote what they considered to be a "sunrise" technology. Tens of billions of dollars have been expended over four decades on government subsidies for research and production of nuclear power plants, equipment, and fuels. It has been a bonanza of cost-plus revenues for the monopoly utility companies that commissioned the plants. It has been a seemingly endless, billion-dollar gravy train for the labor unions and construction trades who built the plants initially, who dismantled them when they constantly had to be redesigned, who constructed them over and over again, and who cheerfully drew their pay all the while. But the consequences for the country should be sobering: astronomical cost overruns, billions of dollars worth of abandoned power plants, multimillion-dollar rate hikes, a hopelessly uneconomic electric power source, a sector that has grown more dependent on government subsidies in order to survive, deception of the public regarding risks and health threats, and a lethal, steadily mounting harvest of radioactive wastes for which no acceptable method of disposal has yet been devised.

Defense weapons procurement is another field where coalition capitalism can be seen in action. Here too, we see close "cooperation" between government, management, and labor—so close, in fact, that the same people literally pass from one side to the other through a well-greased "revolving door" of government and contractor employment. Here too, government and management have collaborated in designing weapons, and in building and buying them. Here too, all involved have come to a tender appreciation of their mutual problems and concerns—as a steady stream of indictments and criminal convictions continually attest. And for the public who pays the bills? Incredible cost overruns; planes that don't fly, tanks that don't run, guns that can't shoot; and ineffective, contrived, and at times nonexistent testing. It is a coalition carnival of $600 hammers and $7,000 coffee pots.

In airlines and trucking, management and organized labor collaborated for decades to cartelize and monopolize under the guise of government regulation "in the public interest." They erected insuperable barriers to new entry. They insulated themselves from new competition. They parceled out routes and divided territories. And the results of these government-created, government-protected industry cartels? Artifically inflated prices and wages far in excess of competitive levels for the dominant firms and organized labor, all at public expense.

In international trade policy, underperforming and noncompetitive corporate giants have joined with organized labor in lobbying government for import restraints on foreign competition. Together with government, they have perfected coalition capitalism into a fine art, in order to protect themselves from the consequences of their own deplorable economic performance, and to continue to play the price-wage-price escalation game. In steel, for example, Big Management and Big Labor have for two decades joined with government to impose restraints, quotas, and tariffs on imported steel—an exercise in coalition capitalism that has inflated steel prices in the American market 20 to 40 percent above world levels, that has handicapped steel-using American firms in international markets, and that has shackled the U.S. economy with excess costs variously estimated as high as $6 billion annually. The American automobile oligopoly, facing its first serious bout of competition since World War II and burdened with a self-inflicted record of inefficiency, technological backwardness, bureaucratic dry rot, and uncompetitive prices and wages, was not to be outdone. In the early 1980s, it too embarked on a course of management-labor-government collaboration and successfully obtained import restraints on high-quality, efficiently produced, fuel-economical Japanese cars. In this case, coalition capitalism operated to raise U.S. new car prices as much as $2,500 per car, and cost American consumers an estimated $5.8 billion yearly.

Surveying the record, an objective observer might well conclude that some of the most serious problems bedeviling the country are due not to too little collaboration, but to too much. Encouraging more of it as a matter of national economic policy would be the essence of folly.

The second defect of coalition capitalism is its misplaced faith in mega-mergers, corporate giantism, and further consolidation of

American industry. It is fatuous to suggest that the problems of the American automobile industry are somehow due to the fact that General Motors is too small when the firm ranks as one of the world's very largest industrial concerns, when it is bigger than its three largest Japanese rivals *combined*, and when a number of informed analysts are now concluding that GM's troubles stem in important part from its excessive size. In its recent cover story (entitled "GM: What Went Wrong?"), *Business Week* concludes that the "basic question nagging this biggest, most diverse, and most integrated of car companies is whether it is just too big to compete in today's fast-changing car market."[11]

Nor can one seriously ascribe the economic shortcomings of the American steel industry to the idea that Big Steel is too little, or that it has been prevented from merging and consolidating, when merger-induced giantism in the industry has proceeded virtually uninterrupted from the formation (through merger) of the United States Steel Corporation in 1901 to the consolidation (and subsequent collapse) of LTV and Republic Steel in the 1980s. Indeed, if giant size, mega-mergers, and oligopoloid concentration were truly conducive to international competitiveness, these firms should be the efficiency and innovation marvels of the world. Obviously they are not.

More generally, the massive turn-of-the-century American merger movement did not produce superior economic performance. Instead, as we have seen, it fueled a speculative financial orgy that ended in panic and economic recession. The furious consolidation and holding company movement of the 1920s hardly unlocked a cornucopia of outstanding economic performance. And the conglomerate merger craze of the 1960s created the corporate giants that failed in the 1970s, and that are being disassembled in the 1980s—scarcely economic progress in any meaningful sense.

Abroad, two decades of merger-induced corporate giantism failed to provide salvation for West European nations imbued with the corporate bigness complex. As we have seen, the "national champions" that they urged to merge during the 1950s and 1960s became the lame ducks of the 1970s and 1980s. They typically have required financial life-support from government in order to forestall outright economic collapse.

Nor can the postwar Japanese miracle be attributed primarily to government-industry collaborationism, induced corporate consolidation, or excessive industry concentration. Rather than any of these, Japan has benefited primarily from an intensely competitive industrial milieu—a competitive domestic economic structure put into place by the Allies following World War II, and one that compels efficiency and innovation, both at home and abroad. In fact, in automobiles, steel, computers, electronics, and machine tools, fiercely independent Japanese producers have vigorously resisted government efforts to merge and consolidate them, as well as government attempts to limit chosen fields to one or a few "national champions."

In automobiles, for example, Honda and other entrepreneurs ignored government efforts to restrict the field to just two firms. As a result, Japan now has nine hotly competitive car companies (compared to three in the United States). In machine tools, the president of one producer recounts that MITI "told us to form into larger companies. We told them 'the hell with that' and refused."[12] In fact, and contrary to popular myth, David Friedman points out that during Japan's high-growth postwar period, "the structure of its manufacturing industries appears to have broadly *diverged* from that of the United States. Japanese production increasingly took place in smaller firms, which employed the vast majority of the country's work force and accounted for close to 60 percent of the national value added. In the United States, by contrast, the number of small firms stabilized as the largest producers employed most of the work force and accounted for close to 65 percent of manufacturing value added."[13] The Japanese, it seems, have succeeded the old-fashioned way—not by elaborate collaboration schemes or by engaging in mega-mergers and hostile takeovers, but by building better products, of higher quality, in modern state-of-the-art facilities, and by striving constantly to produce them more efficiently and more effectively.

In the final analysis, coalition capitalism and "industrial policy" are modern-day reincarnations of the economic syndicalism that was temporarily fashionable in the 1930s. Their Achilles' heel has been most incisively exposed by Henry C. Simons. "Bargaining organizations will contest over the division of the swag," he wrote, "but we commonly overlook the fact that they have large common interests as against the community and that every increase of monopoly power on one side serves to strengthen and implement it on the other." To encourage negotiations and bargaining among organized interest groups as a matter of public policy, Simons warned, would be to "drift rapidly into political organization along functional, occupational lines—into a miscellany of specialized collectivisms, organized to take income away from one another and incapable of acting in their own common interest or in a manner compatible with general prosperity."

The consequences would pose an intractable dilemma for a free society: "If the organized economic groups were left to exercise their monopoly powers without political restraint, the result would be a usurpation of sovereignty by these groups—and, perhaps, a domination of the state by them. On the other hand, if the state undertakes to tolerate (instead of destroying) such organizations and to regulate their regulations, it will have assumed tasks and responsibilities incompatible with its enduring in a democratic form." He concluded that there "can be no sanguine view as to where the proliferation of organization leads."[14]

The record bears out this insight. As a public policy path for improving American economic performance, coalition capitalism is a dead end.

14

CREATIVE CAPITALISM

. . . Come my friends,
'Tis not too late to seek a newer world. . . .
To strive, to seek, to find, and not to yield.
—Tennyson, "Odysseus"

"Greed is good," said Gordon Gekko (Michael Douglas), the wheeler-dealer wizard in *Wall Street*. "Greed is right. Greed works. Greed clarifies, cuts through, and captures the essence of the evolutionary spirit. Greed in all its forms—greed for life, for money, for love, for knowledge—has marked the upward surge of mankind. And greed will not only save [our company], but that other malfunctioning corporation called the U.S.A."

"Greed is all right," Ivan Boesky told the graduating class of the University of California School of Business Administration in 1985. "Greed is healthy. You can be greedy and still feel good about yourself."

"Greed really turns me off," says Henry Kravis, the king of Wall Street's leveraged-buyout strategists.

Who is right? What is the role of greed, the lust for profit, the penchant for self-enrichment—call it what you will—in a free enterprise economy?

In 1776, Adam Smith wrote that self-interest serves a vital function in economic life: "It is not from the benevolence of the butcher, the brewer, or the baker that we expect our dinner, but from their regard for their self-interest. We address ourselves not to their humanity, but to their self-love, and never talk to them of our necessities, but of their advantages." If left free to pursue their animal spirits, Smith counseled, they would automatically—as if guided by an "unseen hand"—not only enrich themselves but, at the same time, increase the wealth of the nation.[1] Private vice would result in public virtue.

However, Smith and his followers also believed that the pursuit of private gain had to be constrained within a framework of rules, so as to harness it to social ends. To them, laissez-faire was not the same as anarchy. They recognized, with Thomas Hobbes, that a state of nature is fraught with "fear and violent death" and that man's life in nature is "poor, nasty, brutish, and short";[2] that good order does not arise from a universal perception of a harmony of interests; that government is not a purely voluntary association; that, on the contrary, good order requires an irreducible element of governmental force, coercion, and intervention to maintain the framework in which freedom can flourish. Harmony and mutuality of interests being neither automatic nor inevitable, it is necessary "to provide and enforce a framework of rules for securing freedom, and the conditions necessary for effective freedom, in economic life."[3] Laissez-faire was a policy prescription not so much for individual freedom as for a free economic system.

To ensure that individual freedom and the private profit motive perform their assigned social task, there must be a rule-maker and an umpire. As (Lord) Lionel Robbins put it: "The invisible hand which guides men to promote ends which were no part of their intention, is not the hand of some god or some natural agency independent of human effort; it is the hand of the lawgiver, the hand which withdraws from the sphere of the pursuit of self-interest those possibilities which do not harmonize with the public good."[4] In the lexicon of the Classicists, the harmony between the pursuit of self-interest and the maximization of general welfare was neither natural, nor spontaneous, nor self-generating.[5]

Economists have long recognized that not all private activity in search of profit is necessarily "productive" from a social point of view. Some 150 years after the publication of *The Wealth of Nations*, John Maynard Keynes elaborated on the distinction between socially productive and unproductive economic activities. He was particularly concerned with the difference between speculation and enterprise, between emphasis on the short-term value of securities and the underlying long-term value of investment. Speculators, he wrote, "are concerned, not with what an investment is really worth to a man who buys it 'for keeps,' but with what the market will value it, under the influence of mass psychology, three months or a year hence."[6] Their private objective is to beat the gun, to outwit the crowd, and "to pass the bad, or depreciating half-crown to the other fellow."[7] For speculators, investment is "a game of Snap, of Old Maid, of Musical Chairs—a pastime in which he is victor who says *Snap* neither too soon nor too late, who passes the Old Maid to his neighbour before the game is over, who secures a chair for himself when the music stops."[8]

Experience shows, Keynes argued, that investment which yields private profit is not necessarily socially advantageous. Indeed, when speculation becomes pervasive, it may inflict serious damage on an economy. It becomes a bane to industrial (that is, socially productive) enterprise: "When the capital development of a country becomes a by-product of the activities of a casino, the job is likely to be ill-done. The measure of success attained by Wall Street, regarded as an institution of which the proper social purpose is to direct new investment into the most profitable channels in terms of future yield, cannot be claimed as one of the outstanding triumphs of *laissez-faire* capitalism—which is not surprising, if I am right in thinking that the best brains of Wall Street have in fact been directed towards a different object."[9]

Clearly there is a need for rules—implemented by carrot or by stick—to channel business activity away from speculation and into productive investment.

The distinction between creative capitalism and speculative capitalism is fundamental. One generates wealth; the other merely redistributes it. One builds factories; the other merely trades their ownership. One gives birth to new goods, services, and techniques; the other merely rearranges control over them. One contributes to economic growth; the other is nothing more than a zero-sum game.

Henry Ford is the personification of creative capitalism. The quintessential industrial entrepreneur and innovator, he had the ability (in Schumpeter's famous phrase) "to see beyond the reach of familiar beacons." In the eyes of the public (and the money interests on Wall Street), he was cantankerous, eccentric, unconventional, and rash. A born maverick, he passionately pursued an idea, a dream, a vision: to make the automobile an article of mass consumption. He had the abiding faith that "every time I reduce the charge for our car by one dollar, I get a thousand new buyers"; that "every time the company cut prices it tapped a new layer of demand; that the number of these successive layers was greater than men supposed; and that as they went lower the layers grew bigger. Further price reductions meant new enlargements of the market, and acceleration of mass production's larger economies, and greater aggregate profits."[10] Its firm grasp of this principle was the company's unique strength.

Ford viewed price reduction and plant expansion as the key to the long-term growth of the company (which he called "the institution"). The institution did not exist to make money, but to create jobs and produce goods. The idea of hoarding money was abhorrent to him. People should use it; they should "invest wisely, to begin getting things that make their lives more productive of real values." His personal profits were tremendous—but they were nearly all reserved for plant expansion, "to build more and more factories, to give as many people as I can a chance to be prosperous."[11] To Ford, money was just "part of the conveyor line." It was just "what we use to keep tally."

Ford was a hands-on industrial entrepreneur par excellence. His office, reported *Detroit Saturday Night* in 1910, "would never remind one of those elegantly furnished headquarters generally ascribed to men of his position. You will find it on the other side of a little obscure door in a corner of the second floor of the factory. He has a little four by six flat desk, and no armchair. In addition, there is a mammoth blackboard, a drafting table, a turret lathe, and several hundred patterns, castings, and samples. It is a workshop, not an office, and is typical of the busy life of the man who has revolutionized automobile conditions the world over. It opens into the tool room, and one is more apt to find him outside busy on some special tool than inside."[12]

The bankers came from a different world. They saw things differently. Sitting in their Wall Street offices, they dealt not in tangible wealth, but in slips of paper symbolizing wealth. They controlled wheat they had not sown, cotton they had not picked, ore they had not mined, steel plants they had not built. They were in the business of producing companies, not goods and services. The dominant financiers of the time saw little promise in the nascent automobile industry, and refused to provide it with capital. At the turn of the century, the eminent financier Chauncey M. Depew, president of the N.Y. Central & Harlem R.R. Co., counseled his nephew against investing $5,000 in the business of an unknown mechanic named Henry Ford. "The horseless carriage," he said, "will never supplant the horse." In 1908, when one of the automobile pioneers told George W. Perkins of J. P. Morgan and Company that "the time will come when five hundred thousand automobiles will be manufactured and sold in this country every year," the banker, incensed by what he took to be Durant's effrontery and stupidity, left the room. He could not foresee the day when Americans would not only want cars, but would virtually mortgage their lives to get one.[13]

No wonder Ford (who financed the growth of his company with capital provided by far-sighted investors in Detroit and later with retained earnings) had a jaundiced view of Wall Street. Bankers, he said, try to shape company policy to pay quick dividends at the cost of future growth, so as to unload stock issues on the public at excessive prices. Bankers "think solely in terms of money. They think of a factory as making money, not goods. They watch the money, not the efficiency of production."[14] They may be successful money-makers, but they "have never added one penny-worth to the wealth of the world." "Does a card player add to the wealth of the world?" Ford asked. His answer was unambiguous: "Speculation in things already produced—that is not business. It is just more or less respectable graft."[15]

Ford was undeterred by the rebuffs of the financial community. He began "with almost nothing." What he earned, he earned "by unremitting labor and faith in a principle." He took what was considered a luxury and turned it into a necessity, and did so "without trick or subterfuge." He built his car (and his company) at a time when the conventional wisdom viewed the automobile as "at the best a rich man's toy."[16] Above all, he never deviated from his conviction that a manufacturer is "an instrument of society and he can serve society only as he manages his enterprises so as to turn over to the public an increasingly better product at an ever-decreasing price, and at the same time to pay to all those who have a hand in his business an ever-increasing wage, based upon the work they do. In this way and in this way alone can a manufacturer or any one in business justify his existence."[17]

Ford expanded by building, not buying. (His only acquisition was the Lincoln Motor Co.) He exemplified what creative capitalism is all about.

Looking back on the entrepreneurial achievements of a Henry Ford, an Andrew Carnegie, a Thomas Alva Edison, or an Alexander Graham Bell, we might be tempted to agree with Emerson's dictum that "once we had golden priests and wooden chalices. Now we have wooden priests and golden chalices." That would be an exaggeration. America is not devoid of innovators and entrepreneurs. Nor does Japan, despite its remarkable achievements, have a monopoly of such talent.

Take, for example, the remarkable exploit of Howard Head, father of the Head ski and the Prince tennis racket, who built a multimillion-dollar business on the basis of a "simple" invention. *Sports Illustrated* tells the story:

> In 1946 Head went off to Stowe, Vt., for his first attempt at skiing. "I was humiliated and disgusted by how badly I skied," he recalls, "and, characteristically, I was inclined to blame it on the equipment, those long, clumsy hickory skis. On my way home I heard myself boasting to an Army officer beside me that I could make a better ski out of aircraft materials than could be made from wood."
>
> Back at Martin [Aircraft], the cryptic doodles that began appearing on Head's drawing board inspired him to scavenge some aluminum from the plant scrap pile. In his off-hours he set up shop on the second floor of a converted stable in an alley near his one-room basement flat. His idea was to make a "metal sandwich" ski consisting of two layers of aluminum with plywood sidewalls and a center filling of honeycombed plastic.
>
> Needing pressure and heat to fuse the materials together, Head concocted a process that would have made Rube Goldberg proud. To achieve the necessary pressure of 15 pounds per square inch, he put the ski mold into a huge rubber bag and then pumped the air out through a tube attached to an old refrigerator compressor that was hooked up backward to produce suction. For heat, he welded together an iron, coffin-like tank, filled it with motor oil drained from automobile crankcases and, using two Sears, Roebuck camp burners, cooked up a smelly 350 degree brew. Then he dumped the rubber bag with the ski mold inside into the tank of boiling oil and sat back like Julia Child waiting for her potato puffs to brown.
>
> Six weeks later, out of the stench and smoke, Head produced his first six pairs of skis and raced off to Stowe to have them tested by the pros. To gauge the ski's camber, an instructor stuck the end of one into the snow and flexed it. It broke. So, eventually, did all six pairs. "Each time one of them broke," says Head, "something inside me snapped with it."
>
> Instead of hanging up his rubber bag, Head quit Martin the day after New Year's 1948, took $6,000 in poker winnings he had

stashed under his bed, and went to work in earnest. Each week he would send a new and improved pair of skis to Neil Robinson, a ski instructor in Bromley, Vt., for testing, and each week Robinson would send them back broken. "If I had known then that it would take 40 versions before the ski was any good, I might have given it up," says Head. "But fortunately, you get trapped into thinking the next design will be it."

Head wrestled with his obsession through three agonizing winters. The refinements were several: steel edges for necessary bite, a plywood core for added strength, and a plastic running service for smoother, ice-free runs. One crisp day in 1950, Head stood in the bowl of Tuckerman's Ravine in New Hampshire and watched ski instructor Clif Taylor come skimming over the lip of the headwall, do a fishtail on the fall line and sweep into a long, graceful curve, swooshing to stop in front of the beaming inventor.

"They're great, Mr. Head, just great," Taylor exclaimed. At that moment, Head says, "I knew deep inside I had it."[18]

Howard Head's credo? "You have to believe in the impossible."

Howard Head is not alone. There is Chester Carlson, inventor of xerography and founder of the Xerox Corporation, which now ranks No. 34 in the Fortune 500.

There is Edwin Land, inventor of the instant camera and founder of the Polaroid Corporation—No. 208 on the *Fortune* list.

There is Kenneth Iverson, president of Nucor, and Gordon Forward, president of Chaparral, innovators of the minimills that have revolutionized a somnolent, lethargic American steel industry.

There is Steve Jobs, the science wizard who in 1976 revolutionized the computer industry with the Apple McIntosh and in 1985 followed that triumph with the equally pathbreaking Next computer.

And then there is the legendary H. Ross Perot, the jug-eared, belt-and-suspenders former naval officer, who left IBM in 1962, founded Electronic Data Systems (EDS) with savings of $1,000, and later sold the company to General Motors for $2.5 *billion*. Although this made him the largest stockholder in General Motors (and a member of its board of directors), Perot found GM's corporate culture unpalatable. He was turned off by the committees, consultants, and MBAs, the corporate dining room, the chauffeured limousines, the hefty bonuses in hard times. At GM, he felt, the order of the day was "ready, aim, aim, aim. . . ." At EDS, the order had been "ready, aim, fire, fire, fire. . . ." He wanted to get back in the trenches with his troops. And so he accepted a "buyout" of his GM stake for $750 million and promptly set up Perot Systems Corp. A can-do entrepreneur, he would start all over again with a dedicated corporal's guard of 75 employees.[19]

These innovator-entrepreneurs illustrate Peter Drucker's observation on creativity in business: "Whenever anything is being accomplished, it is being done . . . by a monomaniac with a mission."[20]

When the priorities are properly ordered, the objective to be attained made clear, and the game to be played specified, latent entrepreneurial talent can be mobilized in even very large, bureaucratic organizations. World War II, when American industry was the arsenal of democracy, provides endless illustrations. Chrysler's contract for army tanks is a case in point: "In June 1940, Chrysler sent a research team to the Rock Island Arsenal to examine tanks and tank blueprints, as Chrysler had never made modern tanks before. Returning to Detroit with 186 pounds of blueprints, Chrysler broke ground for the new plant in September, 1940, and regular production began the following April. Only 10 months had elapsed since Chrysler undertook the project, only 7 months since the plant was actually begun."[21]

Another case of spectacular achievement in a totally foreign field was General Motors' "production of .30 caliber machine guns at their Saginaw Steering Gear Division. A site was selected for the new plant in November, 1940, and the plant was dedicated and began producing on April 22, 1941, a period of six months. By March, 1942, the Saginaw plant had delivered over 28,000 guns on a contract calling for 280 by that date; the price per unit had dropped from $667.00 to $141.44."[22]

These were truly heroic achievements in industrial entrepreneurship—or, more precisely, intrapreneurship. They were feats of creative capitalism.

As a society, we must decide which game we want the business community to play. We must decide between enterprise and speculation; between creating wealth and trading it; between building factories and shuffling corporate paper; between investing in the future or playing an unproductive zero-sum game. Given the right signals, American business can rise to the challenge.

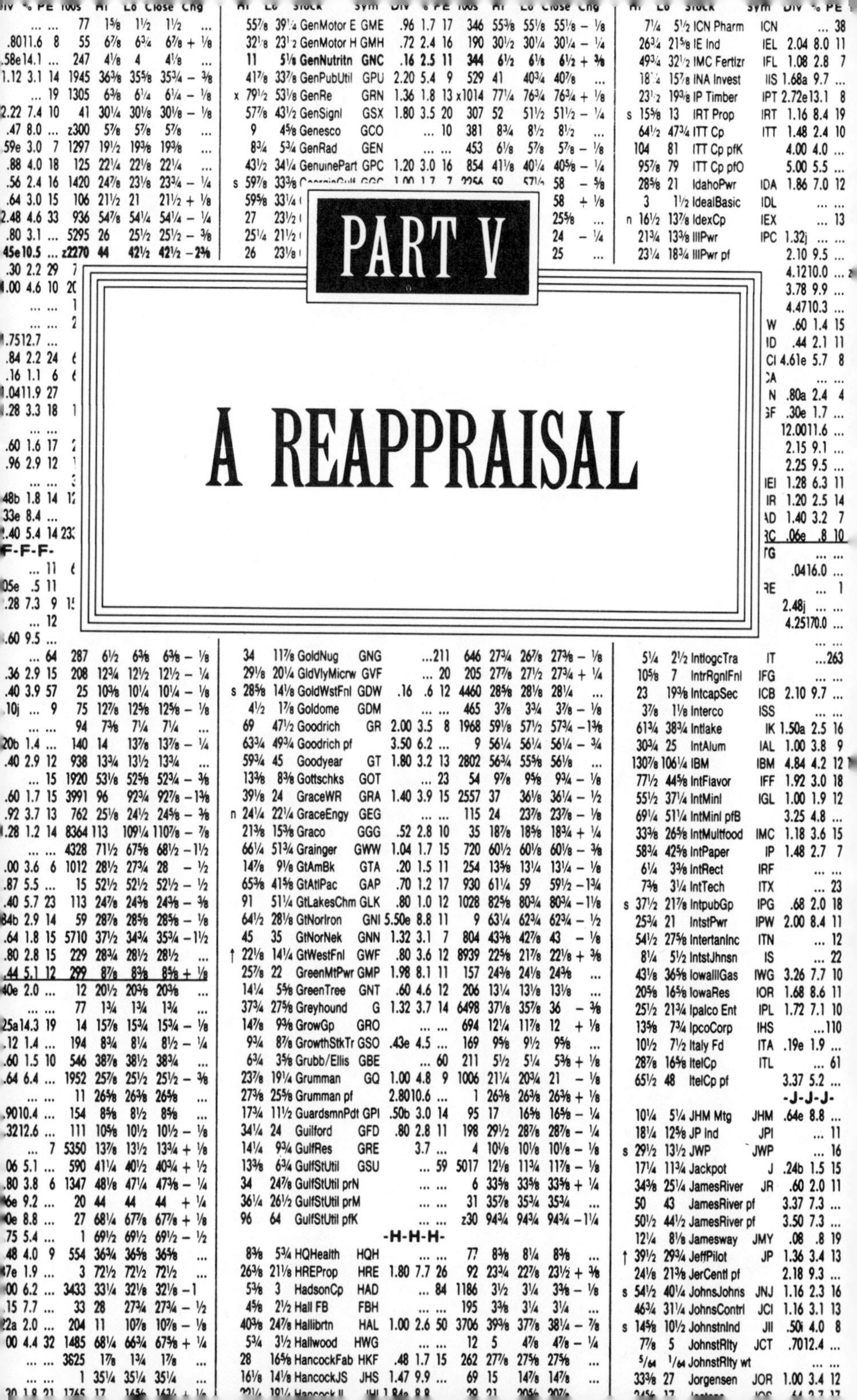

PART V

A REAPPRAISAL

15

CHOOSING THE RIGHT GAME

Each nation takes its place in the history of the world, not merely by its wealth, but by the use that it makes of it. . . .
—William Cunningham,
Growth of English Commerce and Industry, 1903

More than two hundred years ago, Adam Smith observed that "there is one sort of labour which adds to the value of the subject upon which it is bestowed; there is another which has no such effect. The former, as it produces a value, may be called productive; the latter, unproductive labour." The labor of a manufacturer, he stated, is productive because it creates values in the form of "vendible commodities." However, the labor of "both some of the most important, and some of the most frivolous professions" is unproductive of any value. In this category, Smith included churchmen, lawyers, buffoons, musicians, and opera singers. He may be forgiven for not having foreseen the emergence of merger, takeover, and buyout artists.

Today, however, the *danse macabre* goes on. Resources continue to be diverted from productivity-enhancing pursuits into nonproductive paper entrepreneurialism. Increasingly, says Robert Reich, "the most sought-after jobs among business school graduates have been in finance and consulting, where the specialty is rearranging assets and shuffling corporate boxes—and from which bright young MBAs have their best shot at becoming corporate executives."[1] The "best and brightest" in the nation's universities are being lured into graduate programs in law, finance, and accounting, while science and engineering programs are languishing. The United States now has roughly one lawyer for every 400 citizens; in Japan, only one in every 10,000 citizens is trained in the law, but one out of 25 is trained in engineering or science. No wonder James Tobin, Yale's Nobel laureate, voices "uneasy suspicion, perhaps unbecoming an academic, that we're throwing more and more of our resources, including the cream of our youth, into financial activities remote from the production of goods and services, into activities that generate high private rewards disproportionate to their social productivity." David Halberstam calls this diversion of talent "a brain drain" of massive proportions.[2]

But the merger game ensnarling the American economy is not a matter of fate. Nor is it dictated by sunspots or the location of the stars. A nation *chooses* the kind of economic game it plays, as well as the rules by which it is played. A nation chooses, either explicitly or by default, to allow corporate deal-mania to rage. It chooses, explicitly or by default, the kinds of skills it will encourage by virtue of the rewards it provides. A nation also chooses the economic consequences it will have to endure. In the case of the merger game, these consequences include the loss of markets to foreign competitors at home and abroad; stubbornly persistent trade deficits; inadequate capital formation and lagging research and development; declining productivity and hollow, debt-laden corporations; and the acquisition of U.S. production facilities by foreign buyers willing to use them productively.

If these outcomes are unacceptable, and if the nation desires growth in its real productive wealth and in its standard of living, then it must choose to play a different game, with different rules and with a different payoff matrix. It must implement public policies designed to encourage creative capitalism—a game whose objective is real investment in real plants, real products, real innovation, and real state-of-the-art manufacturing techniques. It must implement public policies that will channel skills, energies—and rewards—into real values built on the factory floor and in the research laboratory. It must stop paper entrepreneurship and unleash the forces of productive entrepreneurship.

This can be done in a number of ways, and on a variety of fronts.

1. ELIMINATE INTEREST DEDUCTIONS FOR DEBT. According to influential Wall Street economist Henry Kaufman, "The current system of tax rules and financial regulations sets up a set of incentives and motivations that virtually ordain that the M&A-LBO craze will continue until it threatens the financial condition of the entire corporate sector." What Kaufman calls the "pathology of excessive leverage" is working to decapitalize American industry. "It creates a real threat to the financial vitality of the corporations involved—a threat that will become harshly apparent in the next recession, whenever that may come."[3]

One way to slow down merger madness would be to remove the tax deductibility of interest payments on debt created solely to effect transfers of corporate control. Eliminating this interest deduction would remove the stimulus to corporate deals that the tax code currently provides. It would also discourage the further escalation of already excessive corporate debt, and render the economy less vulnerable to a financial meltdown. To avoid creating an unfair advantage for foreign buyers of American firms, whose home countries may continue to permit such interest expense deductibility, a special tax could easily be imposed on foreign acquisitions and takeovers of U.S. firms.[4]

A less drastic proposal—designed primarily to deal with the proliferation of junk bonds (which Theodore Forstmann calls "the fake wampum of 1980s finance")—would eliminate tax deductions for interest on two kinds of bonds: zero-coupon bonds that pay no interest until maturity and are sold at a deep discount to their face value, and "payment-in-kind," or PIK, bonds that make interest payments in the form of more bonds, rather than in cash. This propsosal, currently under consideration by the House Ways and Means Committee, would only apply to bonds that have a term of more than five years and that pay yields of at least five percentage points more than U.S. Treasury securities of comparable maturity. If enacted, it would reduce the proclivity to incur "junk debt'" to finance mergers, takeovers, and LBOs.

2. TIGHTEN FINANCIAL REGULATIONS ON DEAL-MAKING. In the aftermath of the Great Crash of 1929, and in order to put a cap on financial speculation, Securities and Exchange Commission regulations established strict upper limits (50 percent) on the proportion of stock purchases that individuals are permitted to finance through debt and borrowing. This margin requirement is designed to rein in speculative fever by requiring that individuals back up purchases of corporate securities with tangible real assets worth at least 50 percent of the value of the stock purchase. Applying the same kind of margin requirements to bank borrowings and junk bonds issued for purposes of takeovers and buyouts—and for changes in corporate control generally—would squeeze a considerable degree of speculation out of the capital markets, curb the excessive extensions of credit currently fueling deal-mania, and put corporate financing on a sounder and considerably more sober footing.

At the same time, federal regulations on bank lending can be tightened, and bank loans for highly leveraged corporate deals can be more closely scrutinized by bank regulatory authorities. Loans for corporate deals might be segregated and classified in a special category, where they can be closely watched. The Federal Reserve Board can (as it is beginning to do) explicitly warn bank examiners and supervisors to evaluate borrowers' financial health not just during rosy economic times, but in the event of an economic downturn or even a recession in the economy at large. All banks can be sensitized—repeatedly—to the importance of not compromising sound lending practices merely in order to fatten their fees.[5]

3. A SLIDING CAPITAL GAINS TAX. Quick-buck buying and selling of corporate assets (including corporate stocks) currently generates huge capital gains, sometimes in a matter of days or even hours! A sliding tax on these gains, with the tax rate varying inversely with the time period over which the assets have been held, would further combat financial speculation and deflate merger-mania.

An example of this approach is provided by Edson W. Spencer, chairman of the board of the Ford Foundation, who proposes the following four-part system: Capital gains accrued on assets held for more than 5 years would pay no tax whatsoever. Capital gains on assets held 2 to 5 years would be subject to a tax of 15 percent. Capital gains on assets held 1 to 2 years would be taxed at the rate of 30 percent. And the most speculative capital gains—those from assets held less than 12 months—would be taxed at the highest rate, 50 percent. In this way, Spencer argues, short-term speculation would be penalized, and the attention of all the players would be oriented to longer-term investment and competitiveness.[6] (At the same time, the system would not penalize owners merely selling out their businesses after having spent a lifetime building them up.)

Warren Buffett, legendary manager of the Berkshire-Hathaway investment fund, goes even further. He proposes a 100 percent tax on all profits derived from the sale of stocks held less than one year. He reasons that if this were done, the "substantial brain power and energy now applied to the making of investment decisions that will produce the greatest rewards in a few minutes, days or weeks would be instantly reoriented to decisions promising the greatest long-term rewards." He further points out that under his approach, the "most enticing category of inside information—that relating to take-overs—would become useless."

4. A SALES TAX ON SECURITIES TRANSFERS. Such a tax has been proposed by Lawrence Summers, a Harvard economist, and Victoria Summers, a Boston securities lawyer. A half-percent levy on every securities transaction, they say, would discourage speculation by deal-makers, and would give institutional investors a greater incentive to hold securities for the long haul. It would have the

additional virtue of raising some $12 billion annually for revenue-starved Washington. (Robert Reich, who also favors the half-percent tax, estimates the revenue yield at $10 billion annually.)

This is not a new idea. In the 1930s, John Maynard Keynes was sufficiently worried about "the predominance of speculation over enterprise" to call for a stock transfer tax. While it is hardly a panacea for the structural problems generated by deal-mania, it would help to attenuate the speculative excesses associated with it.

5. ENFORCE THE ANTIMERGER LAW. One important step would be simply to enforce the antimerger law already on the books. The law, and its judicial precedents, are crystal clear: Section 7 of the Clayton Act prohibits any merger or acquisition (including corporate deals of all sorts) where the effect may be to substantially lessen competition, or to tend to create a monopoly, in any line of commerce, in any geographic section of the country. The purpose of the law, as explicitly interpreted by the Supreme Court, is to arrest "mergers at a time when the trend to a lessening of competition in a line of commerce was still in its incipiency." It gives the federal government and the courts "the power to brake this force at its outset and before it gathered momentum." Its core concern is a "rising tide of economic concentration." In the past, the law has been applied to stop mergers, and trends toward mergers, in all kinds of cases, including horizontal deals between direct competitors, vertical deals between firms operating at different stages within the same industry, and conglomerate deals between firms operating in completely unrelated fields.

Most important, when it has been enforced, the law has produced notably beneficial economic effects. For example, in 1958 the government successfully stopped Bethlehem Steel from acquiring Youngstown Sheet & Tube—a proposed merger between the country's 2nd and 5th largest steel concerns. And what was the result? Once the easy path of expansion via merger was blocked, Bethlehem proceeded to do what it formerly had insisted was impossible: It built an entirely new steel works at Burns Harbor, Indiana—"the only integrated green-field blast furnace oxygen converter-rolling mill complex built during the 1960s and 1970s to provide a U.S. counterpart to the modern steel-making capacity growing by leaps and bounds abroad."[7] The net effect was the construction of a new state-of-the-art facility, which enhanced operating efficiency in a technologically backward industry, created new jobs, and afforded steel-buying companies one more source of supply.

One wonders what the state of the American steel industry might be today if the antitrust agencies had blocked the spate of mergers and acquisitions that produced Big Steel, beginning with the United States Steel Corporation in 1901, and continuing to the present day. More generally, one wonders what levels of productivity, growth, efficiency, innovation, and international competitiveness might be possible if the current wave of mergers and deals throughout the economy were redirected to real economic pursuits and away from the shuffling of paper shares.

6. INTERDICT UNPRODUCTIVE MEGA-MERGERS. Yet no matter how conscientiously or zealously they may be enforced, the antitrust laws cannot possibly cope with the speculative deal-mania sweeping the country. A multibillion-dollar leveraged buyout such as Beatrice or RJR-Nabisco, for example, may not constitute an antitrust violation in any narrow technical sense; but it may nevertheless exact a heavy opportunity cost by diverting resources into unproductive uses and thus seriously compromise the national interest.

One remedy would be to require the proponents of any merger, takeover, or buyout beyond a given threshold size—say, $1 billion—to file a public impact statement to accompany the proposed deal. Such a statement would have to show that the deal will enhance production efficiency; that it will stimulate technological progress; that it will promote international competitiveness; and that these goals cannot be achieved in the absence of the proposed deal. Unless this showing can be made, the deal would be banned. The advantage of this approach would be to put the burden of proof squarely on the shoulders of those proposing the deal. It would force them to demonstrate, with probative evidence rather than extravagant public relations hype, that the projected deal is not only in their selfish interest, but in the public interest as well.

Notwithstanding such a requirement, the country's largest corporations would still be permitted to grow to their heart's content, so long as they did so through *internal* expansion—by constructing new plants, developing new products, and creating new jobs. In short, they would have an incentive to grow by building rather than buying, by creating new values rather than acquiring values created by others.

These are only sketchy suggestions for the kinds of rule changes needed to put an end to a rambunctious, helter-skelter, catch-as-catch-can, humpty-dumpty game that is clearly out of control. Other measures may be equally worthy of consideration. Most important, however, in contemplating rule changes is to keep our eye on the ball—to keep in mind what game we should be playing, our reasons for playing it, and the benefits we expect to derive from it.[8]

"The future is longer than the present," says Paul A. Samuelson, the first American to win the Nobel Prize in economics. "After 1989 has been long forgotten, the American people will have a burning concern with where productivity will be in the late 1990s and into the new century. All this involves supply-side economics—not the 1981 snake-oil supply-side economics of Jack Kemp, David Stockman, and Arthur Laffer—but rather the basic supply-side economics that depends on capital formation, scientific knowledge, managerial know-how, and human capital."[9]

Mergers, takeovers, and buyouts are not the means to that end. They involve an exchange of wealth instead of its creation, a trading of ownership titles instead of investment in the future.

Merger-induced "restructuring"—or whatever euphemism its apostles use to justify it—is a zero-sum game. It is not a magic elixir to cure lagging productivity and declining competitiveness in world markets.

The real wealth of nations is made of sterner stuff.

NOTES

PREFACE

1. In interpreting the significance of debt, either public or private, a cautionary note is in order. As Robert Eisner points out (*How Real Is the Federal Deficit?* [New York: Free Press, 1986]), the purpose for which debt is incurred is of crucial importance. See also Robert Heilbroner and Peter Bernstein, *The Debt and the Deficit* (New York: W. W. Norton, 1989). This is a point to which we shall return repeatedly.
2. Benjamin M. Friedman, *Day of Reckoning* (New York: Random House, 1988), p. 29.
3. Alan S. Blinder, "Want to Boost Productivity?" *Business Week*, April 17, 1989, p. 10.
4. Michael L. Dertouzos, Richard K. Lester, and Robert M. Solow (MIT Commission on Industrial Productivity), *Made in America: Regaining the Productive Edge* (Cambridge: MIT Press, 1989), p. 26.
5. *New York Times*, November 4, 1988, p. 29.
6. Henry Kaufman, "Corporate Finance," *Business Month*, March 1989, pp. 82, 81.

7. *New York Times*, February 5, 1989, p. 24E.
8. Edward Gibbon, *The Decline and Fall of the Roman Empire*, Chap. 38.

1. THE GAME

1. Myron Magnet, "The Money Society." *Fortune*, July 6, 1987, p. 26.

2. THE SCOREBOARD

1. Jeff Madrick, *Taking America* (New York: Bantam Books, 1987), pp. 225–233; John Brooks, *The Takeover Game* (New York: Dutton, 1987), pp. 180–181; *Wall Street Journal*, September 24, 1982, p. 23.
2. U.S. Congress, Senate, Committee on the Judiciary, *Hearing: Oil Merger Activity*, 98th Cong., 2nd Sess., 1984, p. 3.
3. U.S. Congress, House, Subcommittee on Fossil and Synthetic Fuels, *Hearings: Oil Industry Mergers*, 98th Cong., 2nd Sess., 1984, p. 5.
4. See Hope Lampert, "Citizen Campeau," *Business Month*, October 1988, pp. 41–46, and *Wall Street Journal*, April 4, 1988, p. 1.
5. *New Yorker*, May 20, 1985, p. 75.
6. *Business Week*, October 26, 1987.
7. *Wall Street Journal*, June 20, 1989, p. A3.
8. *International Herald Tribune*, July 3, 1989, p. 7.
9. Other transnational deals are noteworthy. France's L'Air Liquide, the world's largest producer of industrial gases, bought Big Three Industries, a leading American industrial gas producer. Through its acquisition of Glidden (at the time the 3rd largest paint producer in the United States), the British firm ICI has become the world's largest paint maker. Hoechst, a German chemical group, bought U.S. Celanese. Union Carbide sold its agricultural chemicals operations to Rhone-Poulenc, a leading French producer of agricultural chemicals. Electrolux, the largest producer of appliances in Europe, acquired White Consolidated Industries (formerly the 3rd largest appliance maker in the United States, whose brands include Frigidaire, Kelvinator, and Gibson). B. P. Nutrition, Ltd., Europe's

largest feed company, acquired Purina Mills, the largest commercial feed company in the United States. Unilever and Chesebrough-Ponds—two of the world's largest consumer product firms—have merged. Perrier, the world's largest purveyor of mineral water, acquired five U.S. mineral water concerns, including the largest. Britain's largest glassmaker, Pilkington Brothers, acquired Libbey-Owens-Ford's American glass facilities. And Grand Metropolitan PLC, one of the world's largest distillers, bought Heublein, the 2nd largest producer of wines and spirits in the American market. In late 1988, Grand Met also took over Pillsbury.

10. *Wall Street Journal*, February 25, 1985, p. 54.
11. Martin and Susan Tolchin, *Buying Into America* (New York: Times Books, 1988), pp. 6, 259–260; *Fortune*, February 13, 1989, p. 94.
12. *Mergers & Acquisitions*, May–June 1988.
13. Barrie A. Wigmore, "Speculation and the Crash of 1987." Paper delivered at the annual meetings of the American Economic Association, New York City, December 28, 1988.
14. *Statistical Abstract of the United States*, 1988.
15. Benjamin M. Friedman, *Day of Reckoning* (New York: Random House, 1988), p. 100.
16. John Kenneth Galbraith, "From Stupidity to Cupidity," *The New York Review of Books*, November 24, 1988, p. 13.
17. *New York Times*, December 22, 1988, p. 33.
18. *Insight*, June 15, 1987, p. 12.

3. THE OUTSIDE RAIDERS

1. *New York Times Magazine*, January 29, 1989, p. 34.
2. Taken from Julia Flynn Siler, "Buyout Baron: William F. Farley," *New York Times*, March 5, 1989, p. 6F. See also Connie Bruck, "Billion-Dollar Mind," *New Yorker*, August 7, 1989, pp. 76–88.
3. T. Boone Pickens, Jr., *Boone* (Boston: Houghton Mifflin, 1987), p. 285.
4. Ibid., pp. 275–289.
5. Interview, *National Journal*, November 22, 1986, p. 2846.
6. Council of Economic Advisers, *Economic Report of the President*, February 1985, Chap. 6.

7. *The Raiders of Wall Street* (New York: Stein and Day, 1986), p. 125.
8. Myron Magnet, "The Money Society," *Fortune*, July 6, 1987, p. 28.

4. THE INSIDE RAIDERS

1. *Fortune*, October 3, 1983, p. 70.
2. Ibid., p. 68.
3. *New York Times*, September 6, 1987, Sec. 3, p. 8.
4. *Wall Street Journal*, December 5, 1985, p. 20.
5. Quoted in *Business Week*, December 5, 1988, p. 33.
6. Quoted in *Business Week*, November 7, 1988, p. 33.
7. "The RJR Greedfest Won't Stop LBO Mania For Long," *Business Week*, December 5, 1988, p. 29.
8. *Time*, December 5, 1988, p. 2.
9. Adam Smith, *The Wealth of Nations*, Modern Library edition, p. 700.
10. Adolf A. Berle and Gardiner C. Means, *The Modern Corporation and Private Property* (New York: Harcourt, Brace & World, 1967), rev. ed., p. 116.
11. Ibid., p. 244.
12. Quoted in report on *Leveraged Buyouts and the Pot of Gold: Trends, Public Policy, and Case Studies*, Subcommittee on Oversight and Investigations, Committee on Energy and Commerce, U.S. House of Representatives, 100th Cong., 1st Sess., December 1987, p. 30 [cited hereafter as Report]. For an elaboration of this line of argument, see Frank H. Easterbrook and Daniel R. Rischel, "Corporate Control Transactions," *Yale Law Journal*, March 1982.
13. *Institutional Investor*, December 1986, p. 119.
14. "Where Are the Shareholders' Yachts? But John Kluge Pockets Billions From Metromedia LBO," *Barron's*, August 18, 1986, p. 6.
15. Gary Hector, "Are Shareholders Cheated by LBO's?" *Fortune*, January 19, 1987, p. 100 (emphasis in original). *Fortune* lists other LBOs that have propelled individual executives "to the outer limits of the known universe for executive compensation": "John Pomerantz, chairman of dressmaker Leslie Fay, which went private in an LBO and then changed hands again in a second LBO, netted

$60 million in four years on an initial investment of less than $1 million. Joseph Flannery, chairman of Uniroyal, expects to earn $20 million on an investment of less than $750,000 a year ago. John Purcell, SFN's top executive, made at least $25 million in 18 months on an investment of less than $500,000." (Ibid., p. 98). F. Ross Johnson, the flamboyant chief executive of RJR-Nabisco, who lost out to KKR in his buyout bid for the company, received a generous consolation package: $25.7 million in cash and securities for the RJR stock he owned, plus a golden parachute which provides that his salary and bonuses (totaling $1,736,700 in 1987) will continue through the end of 1991. He will also receive retirement benefits, starting January 1992 (*Wall Street Journal*, December 2, 1988, p. A4).

16. "Fairness of Management Buyouts Needs Evaluation," *Legal Times*, October 16, 1983, p. 15.
17. Report, p. 9.
18. *New York Times*, April 23, 1987, p. D7.
19. "Takeovers and Buyouts Clobber Blue-Chip Bondholders," *Business Week*, November 11, 1985, p. 113.
20. "The Bondholders' Cold New World," *Fortune*, February 27, 1989, p. 83.
21. Ibid. The evidence of declining bond ratings in the wake of leveraged buyouts is dramatic: "Credit quality in 1986 sank to new lows. Downgrades of industrial bonds outnumbered upgrades by a 4.2 to 1 margin. Bond ratings of 33 industrial companies fell to speculative grade from investment grade. The universe of corporate bonds has become increasingly risky. In May 1987, 497 (56 percent) of 893 rated industrial companies were speculative grade, and BB was the median rating category. Five years earlier, an A rating was the median category. Corporate takeovers and defensive maneuvers to thwart them 'have had a profound impact on declining credit quality.' Recapitalizations were [according to Standard and Poor's] 'the most damaging to credit quality.' " (Morey W. McDaniel, "Bondholders and Stockholders," *Journal of Corporation Law*, December 1987, p. 4.)
22. Report, p. 83.

23. *Wall Street Journal*, December 2, 1988, p. B1.
24. Laura Saunders, "How the Government Subsidizes Leveraged Takeovers," *Forbes*, November 28, 1988, p. 192.

5. THE ESTABLISHMENTARIANS

1. Christian Marfels, "Aggregate Concentration in International Perspective: Canada, Federal Republic of Germany, Japan and the United States," in R. S. Khemani, D. M. Shapiro, and W. T. Stanbury, eds., *Mergers, Corporate Concentration and Power in Canada* (Halifax, NS: Institute for Research on Public Policy, 1988).
2. *Cincinnati Enquirer*, July 26, 1987.
3. U.S. Congress, Senate, Subcommittee on Securities of the Committee on Banking, Housing, and Urban Affairs, *Hearings: Impact of Corporate Takeovers*, 99th Cong., 1st Sess., 1985, p. 880.
4. Peter Drucker, *Concept of the Corporation* (New York: New American Library, 1983), 2nd rev. ed., p. 187.
5. R. Meyer, "The Role of Big Business in Achieving National Goals," in David Mermelstein, ed., *Economics: Mainstream Readings and Radical Critiques* (New York: Random House, 1976), p. 81.
6. *Impact of Corporate Takeover Hearings*, pp. 881, 890.
7. Ibid., p. 888.
8. Ibid., p. 1016.
9. U.S. Congress, House, Subcommittee on Monopolies and Commercial Law of the Committee on the Judiciary, *Hearings: Mergers and Acquisitions*, 99th Cong., 1st and 2nd Sess., 1988, p. 15.
10. U.S. Congress, House, Subcommittee on Telecommunications and Finance of the Committee on Energy and Commerce, *Hearing: Impact of Mergers and Acquisitions*, 100th Cong., 1st Sess., 187, p. 58.
11. *Mergers and Acquisitions Hearings*, p. 332.
12. U.S. Congress, Senate, Committee on Banking, Housing, and Urban Affairs, *Hearings: Hostile Takeovers*, 100th Cong., 1st Sess., 1987, p. 130.
13. Ibid., p. 220.
14. *Impact of Corporate Takeovers Hearings*, p. 1015.
15. Richard Darman, "Looking Inward, Looking Outward: Beyond

Tax Populism." Remarks before the Japan Society Conference on Tax Reform in Japan and the United States, New York City, November 7, 1986.

16. J. Patrick Wright, *On a Clear Day You Can See General Motors* (Grosse Point, MI: Wright Enterprises, 1979), p. 100.
17. *Business Month*, June 1988, p. 14.
18. Michael E. Porter, "From Competitive Advantage to Corporate Strategy," *Harvard Business Review*, May–June 1987, pp. 43–59.
19. *Mergers and Acquisitions Hearings*, p. 300.
20. *Wall Street Journal*, January 6, 1986, p. 1.
21. Ibid.
22. *Fortune*, June 6, 1988, p. 78.

6. THE MARRIAGE BROKERS

1. For a general overview, see Paul Hoffman, *The Dealmakers* (Garden City, N.Y.: Doubleday, 1984).
2. *Wall Street Journal*, April 21, 1982, p. 1.
3. Ibid.
4. Connie Bruck, *The Predators' Ball* (New York: Simon & Schuster, 1988); John Brooks, *The Takeover Game* (New York: Dutton, 1987), pp. 100–103; *Business Week*, July 7, 1986, pp. 56–63.
5. *Fortune*, January 20, 1986, p. 20.
6. T. Boone Pickens, *Boone* (Boston: Houghton Mifflin, 1987), p. 151.
7. Peter Petre, "Merger Fees That Bend the Mind," *Fortune*, January 20, 1986, p. 21.
8. John Brooks, *The Takeover Game* (New York: Dutton, 1987), pp. 252–253.
9. Ibid., p. 95.
10. Lee Smith, "The High Rollers of First Boston," *Fortune*, September 6, 1982, p. 60.
11. "Special Report: Deal Mania," *Business Week*, November 24, 1986, p. 80.
12. *New York Times*, November 16, 1986, Sec. 3, p. 8.
13. *Fortune*, January 20, 1986, p. 23.
14. Allan Sloan, "When the Music Stops . . . ," *Forbes*, November 14, 1988, p. 44.

15. *Business Week*, November 24, 1986, p. 80.
16. *Wall Street Journal*, February 3, 1988, p. 10.
17. Richard Phalon, "Fuel for the Flames?," *Forbes*, November 18, 1985, p. 122.
18. *Business Week*, November 24, 1986, p. 80.
19. *Forbes*, November 18, 1985, p. 122.
20. *Fortune*, January 20, 1986, p. 18; *Wall Street Journal*, February 3, 1988, p. 10.
21. *New York Times*, October 4, 1982, p. 21.
22. *Wall Street Journal*, November 8, 1985, p. 6.
23. *New York Times*, April 5, 1988, pp. 25, 28.
24. *New York Times*, November 13, 1988, p. 8.
25. *New York Times*, November 27, 1988, Sec. 4, p. 8.
26. Brooks, p. 253.
27. Frederick Lewis Allen, *The Lords of Creation* (New York: Harper & Bros., 1935), p. 341.
28. Jeff Madrick, *Taking America* (New York: Bantam Books, 1987), p. 194.
29. *New York Times*, November 5, 1988, Sec. 3, p. 19.

7. THE MACRO RECORD

1. David J. Ravenscraft and F. M. Scherer, *Mergers, Sell-Offs, and Economic Efficiency* (Washington, D.C.: The Brookings Institution, 1987), pp. 202–203, 121, 212, 221, 224.
2. Dennis C. Mueller, "The Effects of Conglomerate Mergers," *Journal of Banking & Finance* 1 (December 1977), p. 344.
3. Dennis C. Mueller, "The Case Against Conglomerate Mergers," in Roger D. Blair and Robert F. Lanzillotti, eds., *The Conglomerate Corporation* (Cambridge, Mass.: Oelgeschlager, Gunn & Hain, 1981), p. 71.
4. Dennis C. Mueller, "Mergers and Market Share," *Review of Economics and Statistics* 67 (May 1985), pp. 266–267.
5. U.S. Congress, House, Subcommittee on Monopolies and Commercial Law of the Committee on the Judiciary, *Hearings: Acquisitions and Joint Ventures Among Large Corporations*, 98th Cong., 1st and 2nd Sess., 1985, p. 265.

6. Mark W. Frankena and Paul A. Pautler, "Antitrust Policy For Declining Industries," Bureau of Economics, Federal Trade Commission, October 1985.
7. Louis Lowenstein, *What's Wrong With Wall Street* (New York: Addison-Wesley, 1988), pp. 132–134. At the same time, the weight of the evidence suggests that those who acquire other firms are *not* "supermanagers" able to work economic miracles with the operations they acquire. In fact, just the opposite seems to be true. Surveying the evidence on this score, Harvard economist Richard E. Caves reports that companies "seeking to run acquired business units on average *underperform* [the operations'] previous specialized managers, or at best fail to improve on their records." He further finds "substantial declines in the real productivity of acquired assets" following merger, while the "average acquiring firm at best realizes no net profit on its consolidated assets and may do substantially worse." Richard E. Caves, "Mergers, Takeovers, and Economic Efficiency: Foresight vs. Hindsight," Harvard Institute of Economic Research, Discussion Paper No. 1405, October 1988 (emphasis added). Economist Stephen A. Rhoades finds similar results for mergers and acquisitions in banking. He reports that "acquiring firms *do not* typically acquire poor performers"; he finds "no indication that the average performance of the acquired banking firm before acquisition is improved after acquisition"; and he concludes that his results "clearly question the view that mergers, at least in banking, rid the system of poor performers or generally result in net public benefits in the form of gains in efficiency or significantly improved prices or services." Rhoades, "The Operating Performance of Acquired Firms in Banking Before and After Acquisition," Staff Study, Federal Reserve System, Washington, D.C., April 1986, p. 18.
8. *Wall Street Journal*, September 10, 1984, p. 1.
9. *Forbes*, November 16, 1987, p. 186.
10. *Business Week*, July 7, 1986, p. 82.
11. *Mergers & Acquisitions*, May–June 1987, p. 13.
12. *Forbes*, January 18, 1982, p. 36.
13. Ravenscraft and Scherer, pp. 166, 169.
14. *Business Week*, October 22, 1984, p. 152.

15. *Business Week*, June 3, 1985, p. 88.
16. *The Economist*, April 17, 1982, p. 67, 1985, p. 134.
17. "Why Soap and Pastrami Don't Mix", *Forbes*, December 2, 1985, p. 134.
18. *Business Week*, July 1, 1985, p. 50.
19. *The Economist*, April 23, 1988, p. 14.
20. *Forbes*, November 18, 1985, p. 122.
21. Anthony Downs, *Inside Bureaucracy* (Boston: Little Brown, 1967), p. 160.
22. Quoted in U.S. Congress, Temporary National Economic Committee, Investigation of Concentration of Economic Power, Monograph No. 13, 76th Cong., 3d Sess., 1941, pp. 130–131.
23. "The GM System Is Like a Blanket of Fog," *Fortune*, February 15, 1988, p. 48.
24. "Big Goes Bust," *Economist*, April 17, 1982, p. 67.
25. Tom Peters, *Thriving on Chaos* (New York: Knopf, 1987), p. 20.

8. THE MICRO RECORD

1. Frederick Lewis Allen, *The Great Pierpont Morgan* (New York: Harper & Bros., 1949), pp. 171–172.
2. Andrew Sinclair, *Corsair: The Life of J. Pierpont Morgan* (Boston: Little, Brown, 1981), p. 125.
3. William Z. Ripley, ed., *Trusts, Pools and Corporations* (New York: Ginn, 1916), p. 223.
4. John K. Winkler, *Morgan the Magnificent* (Garden City, N.Y.: Garden City Publishing Co., 1930), p. 215.
5. Ripley, pp. 197, 204–205.
6. Ida M. Tarbell, *The Life of Elbert Gary* (New York: Appleton, 1925), pp. 117–118.
7. Quoted in Louis D. Brandeis, *Business, A Profession* (Boston: Hale, Cushman & Flint, 1933), pp. 232–233.
8. U.S. Congress, House, Subcommittee on the Study of Monopoly Power, *Hearings: Steel*, part 4A, 81st Cong., 2nd Sess., 1950, pp. 117–136. See also Federal Trade Commission, *The Merger Movement: A Summary Report* (Washington, D.C.: 1948), pp. 70–134, and U.S. Congress, House, Select Committee on Small Business, *Hear-*

ing: Steel—Acquisitions, Mergers and Expansion of 12 Major Companies, 1900 to 1950, 81st Cong., 2nd Sess., 1950.

9. Walter Adams and Hans Mueller, "The Steel Industry," in Walter Adams, ed., *The Structure of American Industry* (New York: Macmillan, 1986), 7th ed., p. 80.

10. The disabilities of U.S. Steel's enormous size became apparent almost from the start. Louis Brandeis pointed out that the "facts show that the organization of [U.S. Steel Corp.] arrested the development of the American export trade in steel. . . . From the moment that the Steel Trust got to work, the American iron and steel industry was diverted from natural to unnatural developments. Costs and prices of raw material were inflated; progress toward economy was arrested; retrogression set in and America's rosy chances of annexing the world's export trade were shattered. . . . It is, indeed, a demonstrable fact that the trust has done more harm than good from an American point of view, that it has burdened and handicapped the American steel trade, and incidentally given Britain, Germany and other countries better chances in the race. Last year, 1910, the British iron and steel exports were further in advance of those of America than they were in 1900, the year before the Steel Trust got down to business; while German exports, which were about thirty per cent below those of the United States in 1900, are now something like three hundred percent above them." Brandeis, pp. 226–227.

    Economist Eliot Jones reported similar findings in his monumental study of 1927: "It is evident that the high degree of control which the Steel Corporation had at the time of its organization was being gradually lost," Jones found. "Even in the lines in which it had a quasi-monopolistic position in 1910, it had lost heavily, almost without exception." Eliot Jones, *The Trust Problem in the United States* (New York: Macmillan, 1927), p. 217.

11. Gordon E. Forward, "Wide-Open Management at Chaparral Steel," *Harvard Business Review*, May–June 1986.

12. *Business Week*, November 30, 1968.

13. Ibid.

14. *Forbes*, January 1, 1969.

15. *Business Week*, June 30, 1980.

16. *Fortune*, February 29, 1988, p. 36.
17. Rand V. Araskog, *The ITT Wars* (New York: Henry Holt & Company, 1989), p. 3; Geoffrey Colvin, "The De-Geneening of ITT," *Fortune*, January 11, 1982, p. 34; and *Wall Street Journal*, June 5, 1986, p. 51.
18. *Business Week*, July 1, 1985.
19. *Forbes*, August 8, 1988; *Business Week*, September 16, 1985; and *New York Times*, January 5, 1987.
20. *Forbes*, October 6, 1986, p. 126.
21. See Gregg Easterbrook, "Lorenzo Braves the Air Wars," *New York Times Sunday Magazine*, November 29, 1987; Michael Ennis, "Sky King," *Business Month*, September 1988; and Thomas Donlan, "Turbulent Trip," *Barron's*, June 8, 1987.
22. Donlan, "Turbulent Trip."
23. Walter Adams and James W. Brock, *The Bigness Complex*, (New York: Pantheon, 1987), Chap. 17.
24. For details, see Walter Adams and James W. Brock, "Reaganomics and the Transmogrification of Merger Policy," *Antitrust Bulletin* 33 (Summer 1988), pp. 351–358.
25. Airline Economics, Inc., "Airline Quarterly," Spring 1988, p. 24.
26. In their carefully documented study, economists Richard Butler and John Huston found that discounted fares to St. Louis rose 45 percent following the TWA-Ozark merger, while unrestricted (or full) fares rose 13 percent. "The Effects of Fortress Hubs on Airline Fares and Service: The Early Returns," *The Logistics and Transportation Review*, 24 (September 1988).
27. *Wall Street Journal*, March 10, 1989, p. A8.
28. *International Herald Tribune*, July 6, 1989, p. 5.
29. See, for example, Robert Kuttner, "Plane Truth," *New Republic*, July 17, 1989, p. 21.

9. THE SMALL INVESTOR

1. *Business Week*, January 12, 1987, p. 39.
2. Ellen B. Magenheim and Dennis C. Mueller, "Are Acquiring-Firm Shareholders Better Off After an Acquisition?" in John C. Coffee, Louis Lowenstein, and Susan Rose-Ackerman, eds., *Knights, Raiders*

and Targets (New York: Oxford University Press, 1988), pp. 180–182.

3. Michael C. Jensen and Richard S. Ruback, "The Market For Corporate Control," *Journal of Financial Economics* 11 (1983), p. 20.
4. Murray Weidenbaum and Steven Vogt, "Takeovers and Stockholders: Winners and Losers," Center for the Study of American Business, Pub. No. 83 (December 1987), p. 6.
5. John Brooks, *The Takeover Game* (New York: Putnam, 1987), p. 143.
6. *New York Times*, March 11, 1987, p. 1.
7. *New York Times*, April 23, 1987.
8. *Wall Street Journal*, January 2, 1987, p. 1.
9. *Business Week*, October 10, 1988, p. 46.
10. *Barron's*, November 24, 1986, p. 9.
11. "Top Aides at Time, Warner Stand to Reap Big Benefits from Merger," *Wall Street Journal*, March 15, 1989, p. A3.
12. *Wall Street Journal*, August 12, 1985, p. 2.
13. *New York Times*, January 26, 1986, Sec. 3, p. 1.
14. Ibid.
15. *Fortune*, January 19, 1987, p. 98.
16. Frederick Lewis Allen, *The Lords of Creation* (New York: Harper & Bros., 1935), p. 358.
17. Richard B. DuBoff and Edward S. Herman, "The Promotional-Financial Dynamic of Merger Movements: A Historical Perspective." *Journal of Economic Issues* 23 (March 1989), p. 107.

10. THE CASINO SOCIETY

1. "Why Pastrami and Soap Didn't Mix," *Forbes*, December 2, 1985, p. 134.
2. Ibid., p. 138.
3. Ibid., p. 134.
4. *Corporate Initiative*, Oversight Hearing before the Subcommittee on Monopolies and Commercial Law, House Judiciary Committee, 97th Cong., 1st Sess., 1981, p. 58.
5. Ibid., p. 61. For an elaboration of this point, see Robert B. Reich,

The Next American Frontier (New York: Times Books, 1983), pp. 140–72.

6. Michael L. Dertouzos, Richard K. Lester, and Robert M. Solow (MIT Commission on Industrial Productivity), *Made in America: Regaining the Productive Edge* (Cambridge: MIT Press, 1989), p. 62.
7. *Business Week*, July 1, 1985, p. 53.
8. Quoted in Willard F. Mueller, "Conglomerates: A Non-Industry," in Walter Adams, ed., *The Structure of American Industry* (New York: Macmillan, 1986), 7th ed., p. 357.
9. For an elaboration of this theme, see Walter Adams and James W. Brock, *The Bigness Complex* (New York: Pantheon, 1987), Chap. 5. See also Ira Magaziner and Mark Patinkin, *The Silent War* (New York: Random House, 1989), and Bennett Harrison and Barry Bluestone, *The Great U-Turn* (New York: Basic Books, 1988).
10. Jack Willoughby, "What a Raider Hath Wrought," *Forbes*, March 23, 1987, p. 56.
11. Ibid.
12. *Wall Street Journal*, December 21, 1988, p. 33.
13. *Fortune*, March 13, 1989, p. 98.
14. Ibid.
15. Gene Koretz, "Business Talks a Better R&D Game Than It Plays," *Business Week*, August 21, 1989, p. 20.

11. THE SANTAYANA CURSE

1. "Merger Mania Is Sweeping Europe," *Fortune*, December 19, 1988, p. 157.
2. Quoted, ibid.
3. Malcolm Baldrige, "The Administration's Legislative Proposal and Its Ramifications," *Antitrust Law Journal* (1986), p. 34.
4. U.S. Congress, Senate, Committee on the Judiciary, *Hearings: Merger Law Reform*, 99th Cong., 2nd Sess., 1986, p. 22.
5. "Executives Support Large Mergers to Counter Foreign Competition," *Wall Street Journal*, March 9, 1984, p. 33; "Making Mergers Even Easier," *New York Times*, November 10, 1985, Sec. 3, p. 1.
6. "Europe's Love Affair With Bigness," *Fortune*, March 1970, p. 95.

This section on the European experience is adapted from Walter Adams and James W. Brock, "The Bigness Mystique and the Merger Policy Debate: An International Perspective," *Northwestern Journal of International Law and Business* #9 (Spring 1988).

7. *The American Challenge* (1968), pp. 24, 53, 67, 153, 159, 160.
8. *Economist*, March 15, 1988, p. 12.
9. *Economist*, March 5, 1977, p. 88.
10. *Economist*, May 23, 1981, pp. 28 and 33.
11. F. M. Scherer, *Industrial Market Structure and Economic Performance* (Chicago: Rand McNally, 1980), 2nd ed., p. 119.
12. Eliot Jones, *The Trust Problem in the United States* (New York: Macmillan, 1927), pp. 38–43.
13. Frederick Lewis Allen, *The Lords of Creation* (New York: Harper & Bros., 1935), p. 10.
14. Ibid.
15. Jones, pp. 288–289.
16. Allen, p. 71.
17. Jones, pp. 538–541.
18. Thomas C. Cochran and William Miller, *The Age of Enterprise* (New York: Harper & Row, 1961), rev. ed., p. 197.
19. Shaw Livermore, "The Success of Industrial Mergers," *Quarterly Journal of Economics* 50 (1935–36), pp. 87–88.
20. Cochran and Miller, pp. 198–199.
21. Allen, pp. 72–73; Cochran and Miller, p. 195.
22. John Kenneth Galbraith, *The Great Crash* (Boston: Houghton Mifflin, 1954), p. 27.
23. Allen, p. 242.
24. Scherer, p. 122, and George J. Stigler "Monopoly and Oligopoly by Merger," *American Economic Review* 60 (May 1950), p. 32.
25. Allen, pp. 247, 266.
26. Ibid., pp. 276–277.
27. Ibid., p. 336.
28. Galbraith, p. 84.
29. Allen, pp. 403–404.
30. Ibid., p. 259.
31. Quoted in Galbraith, p. 19.

32. Quoted in ibid., p. 44.
33. John Kenneth Galbraith, "From Stupidity to Cupidity," *The New York Review of Books*, November 24, 1988, pp. 12–14.
34. Galbraith, *The Great Crash*, pp. 183–184.

12. COWBOY CAPITALISM

1. Robert H. Bork, *The Antitrust Paradox* (New York: Basic Books, 1978), p. 118.
2. U.S. Congress, House, Subcommittee on Telecommunications and Finance of the Committee on Energy and Commerce, *Hearing: Impact of Mergers and Acquisitions*, 100th Cong., 1st Sess., 1987, pp. 131–139.
3. Bork, pp. 205–206.
4. *Nation's Business*, October 1981, p. 59.
5. Daniel Oliver, Address to the Antitrust Law Section of the American Bar Association, New York City, August 12, 1986, reprinted in Commerce Clearing House, *1986 Trade Regulation Reports*, par. 50,481.
6. See Walter Adams and James W. Brock, "Reaganomics and the Transmogrification of Merger Policy," *Antitrust Bulletin*, Summer 1988.
7. *The Works of Jeremy Bentham*, vol. 3, ed. J. Bowring (1962), p. 185.
8. Thomas Hobbes, *Leviathan* (Baltimore: Penguin Books), pp. 185–186.
9. John B. Clark, *The Control of Trusts* (New York: Macmillan, 1912), pp. 200–201.
10. Richard T. Ely, *Studies in the Evolution of Industrial Society* (New York: Grosset & Dunlap, 1903), p. 231.
11. See Walter Adams and James W. Brock, "Corporate Size and the Bailout Factor," *Journal of Economic Issues*, December 1986.
12. *Challenge*, November–December 1986, p. 63.
13. John Maynard Keynes, *The General Theory of Employment, Interest and Money* (New York: Harcourt, 1936), p. 159.
14. For an examination of the cumulative deterioration of one of America's premier tool machine makers, wrought first by a conglomerate acquisition, followed by a debt-crushing LBO, see Max

Holland, *When the Machine Stopped* (Boston: Harvard Business School Press, 1989).

15. John Dewey, *Individualism Old and New* (New York: Minton, Balch & Co., 1930), p. 55.

13. COALITION CAPITALISM

1. U.S. Congress, House, Subcommittee on Economic Stabilization of the Committee on Banking, Finance and Urban Affairs, *Hearings: Industrial Policy*, part 1, 98th Cong., 1st Sess., 1983, pp. 173–178.
2. Lester C. Thurow, *The Zero-Sum Solution* (New York: Simon and Schuster, 1985), p. 263.
3. Ibid., pp. 265–266.
4. Lester C. Thurow, "Abolish the Antitrust Laws," *Dun's Review*, February 1981, p. 72.
5. Joseph L. Bower, "The Case for Building More IBMs," *New York Times*, February 16, 1986, Sec. 3, p. 2.
6. Thurow, *Zero-Sum Solution*, p. 182.
7. Ibid., p. 270.
8. See Walter Adams and James W. Brock, *The Bigness Complex* (New York: Pantheon, 1986), esp. Chaps. 16–18, 20–21, 23, 25.
9. Quoted in Leverett S. Lyon et al., *The National Recovery Administration: An Analysis and Appraisal* (Washington, D.C.: The Brookings Institution, 1935), p. 709.
10. Clair Wilcox, *Public Policies Toward Business* (Homewood, Ill.: Richard D. Irwin, 1971), p. 680.
11. *Business Week*, March 16, 1987, p. 110.
12. Generally, Walter Adams and James W. Brock, "The Bigness Mystique and the Merger Policy Debate: An International Perspective," *Northwestern Journal of International Law and Business* 9 (Spring 1988).
13. David Friedman, *The Misunderstood Miracle* (Ithaca, N.Y.: Cornell University Press, 1988), pp. 9–10.
14. Henry C. Simons, *Economic Policy for a Free Society* (Chicago: University of Chicago Press, 1948), pp. 43–44, 119, 219.

14. CREATIVE CAPITALISM

1. Adam Smith, *The Wealth of Nations* (Modern Library ed.), pp. 14, 423.
2. Thomas Hobbes, *Leviathan* (Baltimore: Penguin Books), p. 186.
3. Frank H. Knight, *Freedom and Reform* (New York: Harper Bros., 1947), p. 205.
4. Lionel Robbins, *The Theory of Economic Policy in English Political Economy* (London: Macmillan, 1952), p. 56.
5. Smith, pp. 314–315.
6. John M. Keynes, *The General Theory of Employment, Interest and Money* (New York: Harcourt, 1936), pp. 154–155.
7. Ibid.
8. Ibid., p. 156.
9. Ibid., p. 159.
10. Allan Nevins, *Ford: The Times, The Man, The Company* (New York: Scribner's, 1954), pp. 492–493.
11. Ibid., pp. 575–576.
12. January 8, 1910; quoted in Nevins, p. 496.
13. David L. Cohn, *Combustion on Wheels* (Boston: Houghton Mifflin, 1944), p. 114.
14. Henry Ford, *My Life and Work* (New York: Doubleday, 1926), p. 176.
15. Ibid., p. 7.
16. Ibid., p. 272.
17. Ibid., p. 135.
18. Quoted in Thomas J. Peters and Robert H. Waterman, Jr., *In Search of Excellence* (New York: Harper & Row, 1982), pp. 202–203.
19. "The Hottest Entrepreneur in America," *INC.*, January 1989. For an incisive examination of the Perot-GM affair, see Doran P. Levin, *Irreconcilable Differences: Ross Perot versus General Motors* (Boston: Little, Brown, 1989).
20. Quoted in Peters, p. 225.
21. John B. Rae, *The American Automobile: A Brief History* (Chicago: University of Chicago Press, 1965), p. 146.
22. Donald Nelson, *Arsenal of Democracy*, p. 226.

15. CHOOSING THE RIGHT GAME

1. Robert B. Reich, *The Next American Frontier* (New York: Times Books, 1983), p. 159.
2. Tobin quoted in Ann Crittenden, "The Age of 'Me-First' Management," *New York Times*, August 19, 1984, Sec. 3, p. 13; David Halberstam, *The Reckoning* (New York: Morrow, 1986), p. 679.
3. *Business Month*, March 1989, pp. 81–83.
4. "Leveraged Buyouts: America Pays the Price," *New York Times Sunday Magazine*, January 29, 1989, p. 40.
5. "Fed Tightens Rules for Banks on LBO Loans," *New York Times*, February 22, 1989, p. A4.
6. *Wall Street Journal*, January 27, 1989, p. A10.
7. F. M. Scherer, *Industrial Market Structure and Economic Performance*, (Chicago: Rand McNally, 1980), 2nd ed., p. 546.
8. It would be unrealistic and imprudent, however, to overestimate the prospects for the requisite *structural* reform. "The problem," says Ralph Nader, "is that the immediate sensory perceptions of people are pretty comfortable. And where they're not comfortable, what I call the 'anestheisa' is operating. People are irritated by pollution, but they have air-conditioning. People are irritated at unemployment, but they have unemployment compensation. There are a whole host of these 'anesthesias' that let people tolerate structural abuses. I'll tell you what the *real* problem is," he says, considering the challenges of the past decade less than those of the coming one: "We ask people to think, instead of asking them to believe. And history has always gone to those who ask people to believe." *(New York Times Sunday Magazine*, January 18, 1976, p. 52.)
9. Paul A. Samuelson, "Outlook for the American and World Economy." Address at Trinity University, San Antonio, Texas, February 9, 1989.

INDEX

PEOPLE

SUBJECTS

ABOUT THE AUTHORS

WALTER ADAMS is former President of Michigan State University, where he is now Distinguished University Professor of Economics. He has taught at the universities of Paris, Grenoble, and Ancona, the Salzburg and Falkenstein Seminars, and the Industrial College of the Armed Forces. He has served on presidential commissions during the Eisenhower, Kennedy, and Johnson administrations, and has frequently appeared as an expert witness before congressional committees. He holds several honorary degrees. His previous books include *Monopoly in America* (1955), *Is the World Our Campus?* (1960), *The Brain Drain* (1968), *The Structure of American Industry* (7th ed., 1986), and, with James W. Brock, *The Bigness Complex* (1986).

JAMES W. BROCK is Professor of Economics at Miami University in Ohio. A popular teacher and a prolific writer, he has contributed articles to diverse professional journals, including the *Quarterly Journal of Economics and Business*, *Journal of Post-Keynesian Economics*, *Challenge*, *California Law Review*, *New York University Law Review*, *Nebraska Law Review*, *Northwestern Journal of International Law and Business*, *Wake Forest Law Review*, *Antitrust Bulletin*, *American Business Law Journal*, *Wirtschaftswoche*, and *L'Industria*. He has testified before congressional committees on both the state and federal levels. He is the co-author of *The Bigness Complex*, which was selected by *Business Week* as one of the ten best business books of 1987.